T0043980

Walk Out of
YOUR
MESS

Books by Samuel Rodriguez

Persevere with Power

Power for Your Day Devotional

Your Mess, God's Miracle

Your Mess, God's Miracle Study Guide

Walk Out of Your Mess

Walk Out of
YOUR
MESS

*40 Days to Seeing God's Miracles
at Work in Your Life*

SAMUEL RODRIGUEZ

Chosen
a division of Baker Publishing Group
Minneapolis, Minnesota

Published by Chosen Books
Minneapolis, Minnesota
www.chosenbooks.com

Chosen Books is a division of
Baker Publishing Group, Grand Rapids, Michigan

Printed in the United States of America

ISBN 978-0-8007-6348-0 (cloth)
ISBN 978-1-4934-4237-9 (ebook)

Library of Congress Cataloging-in-Publication Control Number: 2023028498

24 25 26 27 28 29 30   7 6 5 4 3 2 1

To all the societal architects and cultural reformers
determined to see every single mess become
a miracle in Jesus' name!

Introduction

When life gets messy, it's hard to see clearly.

You want to believe God is at work in your life, but the dirt, distractions and destructions of unexpected events, complicated relationships and painful disappointments can blind you. During these times you try to stay focused on your relationship with God, but too many obstacles block your line of vision. Unable to see clearly what matters most, you eventually lose your sense of direction. You begin to feel stuck or to stumble in shadows.

Which is why it's important to keep your eyes on Jesus.

While you may trust your eyes for taking in what's visible around you, God's Word makes it clear that spiritual vision comes from trusting the Lord, relying on His Spirit and fixing the eyes of your heart on Jesus. In other words, just because you cannot see what God is doing in your life, it does not mean He is not actively transforming your mess into His miracle. Perhaps no other scene in Scripture illustrates this truth as powerfully as an encounter Jesus had with someone who could not see clearly—or in this case, literally could not see at all.

In John 9, Jesus and His disciples crossed paths with a man blind since birth. Surely this man, whose eyes had not functioned properly since birth, must have assumed there was no hope that he would ever see. So often it's hard to expect to receive something you've never had or experienced before. Most likely, the blind man had no reason to expect differently that day—until Jesus entered his life.

Based on the questions the disciples asked Jesus— "Is it this man's fault that he's blind? Or is he being punished for the sins of his parents?"—the blind man probably carried a burden of shame for his condition (John 9:2). But Jesus corrected such faulty thinking:

"Neither this man nor his parents sinned, but this happened so that the works of God might be displayed in him" (John 9:3). Jesus then proceeded to spit on the ground, mix a mud paste and smear it over the blind man's eyes before instructing him to go and wash in a nearby pool. Obeying the Lord, this man saw what he had never seen before!

The blind man's condition was not a punishment or even the consequence of anyone's sin—it was an opportunity for God's power, glory and goodness to be showcased! The answer Jesus gave to the disciples reframed the way they perceived the blind man's condition—and it continues to shift the paradigm of our perception today.

What if the suffering, pain and struggles you're facing are similar to the blind man's condition—not an injustice to endure, but an opportunity to showcase God's glory? Have you ever considered that you're not being punished when faced with challenges but presented with the potential for experiencing the miraculous, omnipotent power of God? The messiness of your life is actually the opportunity for God's miracle!

This devotional collection is based on my book *Your Mess, God's Miracle* and is designed to help you experience more of God's power in the midst of life's messiness. Each day's entry includes:

Your Daily Vision—a key principle or lesson of truth you can apply to your own life based on the blind man's encounter with Jesus.

Your Daily Reading—an exploration of the Daily Vision based on my examination of God's Word and my findings in *Your Mess, God's Miracle*.

Your Daily Scripture—a thematically related and curated verse or brief passage from God's Word to empower you with the clarity of spiritual truth.

Your Daily Prayer Starter—a few sentences to lead you into God's presence as you share your heart in prayer with your heavenly Father.

While each of the forty days builds on the others, the goal is for you to grow deeper in your faith as you focus your gaze on Jesus and envision your life from an eternal perspective. I pray that as God's Spirit changes the way you see, you will experience renewed hope, abundant joy, abiding peace and limitless power on every page for every day.

Are you ready to see what you have never seen before? To experience what you have never experienced before? To go where you have never gone before? My friend, no matter what you're facing—injury, cancer, bankruptcy, divorce, addiction, homelessness, betrayal—nothing is impossible for God!

God wants to give you sight to see what you have never seen before! Right now as you are reading these words, He is birthing a miracle in the midst of your mess. From the spit and mud of your life, get ready to discover His priceless gift. Remove the blindfold and take off your mask. Recognize the areas of blindness that are being transformed.

Open your eyes to what you have never seen before!

—Samuel Rodriguez

day

1

Our God not only helps us see clearly.
Our God helps us see what we've never seen before!

Seeing clearly requires more than just the physical development of your eyes.

While physical vision develops over the first two years of life in most healthy people, there are other ways to see—intellectually, emotionally and spiritually to name a few. Seeing intellectually usually means you're good at observing, comprehending and categorizing the sensory data relayed to your brain. This kind of perception means you "get it," seeing connections and patterns that lead to accurate conclusions based on your personal experiences and past knowledge.

Seeing through an emotional lens allows you to feel empathy, show compassion and express care and concern regarding your own needs and the needs of those around you. You may have heard of emotional intelligence, which helps you see and recognize the often-complex layers of facts and feelings in a given relationship, event or situation. Emotional sight helps you read what is being communicated beyond words spoken and their meaning.

Seeing spiritually provides clarity of vision for what cannot be seen physically, intellectually and emotionally. Spiritual sight requires trusting God and walking by faith, a way of seeing that matures as we grow more reliant on the Holy Spirit in all areas of our lives. This kind of sight requires awareness of what usually cannot be observed by our human faculties. God's Word tells us, "Now faith is confidence in what we hope for and assurance about what we do not see" (Hebrews 11:1). In other words, you don't need 20/20 vision using your eyes to develop faith, wisdom and discernment.

Simply put, the clarity and accuracy of your spiritual vision relies on your relationship with Jesus Christ. Perhaps no encounter in the Bible illustrates this as beautifully as the one found in John 9:1–7. While walking with His disciples one day, Jesus came upon a man blind since birth. Aware of his lifelong condition, the disciples asked their Master if sin—either the man's or his parents'—caused his blindness. In response, Jesus said, "Neither this man nor his parents sinned, but this happened so that the works of God might be displayed in him" (John 9:3).

While His answer probably surprised those listening, what Jesus did next likely amazed them even more. He spit on the ground, made mud with His saliva and the dirt and then spread the mud over the blind man's eyes. Once the blind man's eyes were caked with this mud mask, Jesus told him to go and wash himself in the nearby Pool of Siloam. The man went there, washed and returned *seeing*!

This encounter is more than factual history about a specific miracle of Jesus. When applied to your life today, you can glimpse a paradigm for how God often chooses to meet you in the muck and mire of your greatest trials and produce a miracle of healing and wholeness. Because no matter how big your mess may be, nothing is beyond the Master's ability to make it His miracle!

SCRIPTURE

"Though you have not seen him, you love him; and even though you do not see him now, you believe in him and are filled with an inexpressible and glorious joy, for you are receiving the end result of your faith, the salvation of your souls" (1 Peter 1:8–9).

—— *Prayer* ——

Lord, I am so grateful for the many ways You allow me to see. Thank You for meeting me in the messiness of my life, during those times when I'm not seeing clearly, and producing Your miracle from my mess. Amen.

Spiritual blindness occurs anytime you take your eyes off Jesus. If you want to grow in your relationship with God, then you must be willing to eliminate these blind spots.

You may have heard your areas of weakness, unself-awareness and inattention described as blind spots. Sometimes our blind spots cause us to get blindsided by unexpected events or painful circumstances. We believe that if we had been more obedient, more diligent or more focused, then we likely would not have been caught so off guard. But no matter how well we may think we see what's going on in our lives, no one can see everything going on at all times—at least not with our human senses.

Perhaps you have felt blindsided by the betrayal of a trusted friend or the loss of your job despite overall excellent performance. Discovering the addiction of a loved one can blindside you, as well as finding out your spouse has been unfaithful. It might be a routine doctor's visit that blindsides you with a devastating diagnosis or the progression of a minor health problem into a major concern.

At other times when you feel blindsided, you may have realized later that you were simply unwilling to see what was literally right in front of you. Whether out of fear, uncertainty, denial or an attempt to control your life, you ignored the signs and signals of pending problems. Looking back, you realize that you had ignored what your body had been trying to tell you prior to your doctor's bad news. In hindsight you see that your role at work was eliminated by shifting market trends. Too late you know that your spouse's betrayal did not happen overnight—you had ignored the growing distance in your relationship for some time.

Despite accepting Jesus into your life and welcoming His Holy Spirit to dwell in you, there may be times when you still experience times of blindness. Moments when you overlook the truth in order to justify giving in to temptation. Days when you tell yourself there are no consequences for the secrets you keep. Times when you can't see how leaving church has caused you to drift in your relationship with God.

The encounter between Jesus and the blind man in John 9 reminds us to examine our blind spots and to exercise our spiritual vision as much as possible. Blindness is a condition that anyone can experience when they take their eyes off Jesus. When succeeding at work eclipses your commitment to loving and serving your family the way you know God wants you to do, you're no longer seeing clearly. When focusing on your status and popularity on social media consumes the time you once spent with Him in prayer, you've grown blind to what matters most. When pursuing money or obsessing over what you don't have overshadows gratitude for the many blessings God continues to pour into your life, you no longer see His present goodness.

Before you can experience God's miracle in your mess, you must be willing to see the mess you've been ignoring. You must see what's in front of you before you can see what's beyond.

SCRIPTURE

"I pray that the eyes of your heart may be enlightened in order that you may know the hope to which he has called you" (Ephesians 1:18).

—————————— *Prayer* ——————————

God, I know there are things in my life I have not been able to see, as well as those things I have not wanted to see. Give me courage to seek Your truth about what I've been afraid and unwilling to face. Show me my blind spots and meet me in my messiest moments. Amen.

When you know who you are in Christ, then you will never be blinded by old labels and the devil's lies. Your identity in Christ will bring an end to your spiritual blindness in life!

Anytime you lose sight of God, the devil will try to blind you to the truth. Because once you're not focused on the truth of who God is and the truth of His Word, then the enemy can tempt you into perceiving his lies and false claims as truth. "The god of this age has blinded the minds of unbelievers, so that they cannot see the light of the gospel that displays the glory of Christ, who is the image of God" (2 Corinthians 4:4).

One of the most effective ways the enemy attempts to blind you is with despair. If he can convince you—or influence you to convince yourself—that your situation is hopeless, then he knows your spiritual vision has been impaired. And when your spiritual vision is obscured, then you eventually lose hope.

For example, when you can't see any way for your marriage to be healed, the enemy is blindfolding you. When you no longer envision seeing your loved one beat her addiction, the enemy is blinding you with despair. When you're ready to quit trying financially because you believe you can never get out of debt, that's the devil eclipsing the truth. When your doctors have tried all medications and treatments with no success, then Satan wants you to believe that your body will never be healed.

Another method the enemy uses to blind you is through shame and false guilt. This is not the holy conviction of a healthy conscience arising from the Holy Spirit in you. No, the enemy wants you feeling guilt unnecessarily, even after you have asked for forgiveness and received it from God and those you've offended. Satan wants to darken what you see with a screen of shame that leaves you feeling worthless and unforgivable. The devil tells you that you're a liar, a thief, a gossip, a cheater, a fornicator, an adulterer, a murderer, a hopeless mess who can never be loved or redeemed.

But this simply is not true!

Old labels may have reflected some of your past behaviors, but they can never define you once you've experienced the grace of God and the indwelling power of the Holy Spirit. The Bible makes it clear: "And such were some of you. But you were washed, you were sanctified, you were justified in the name of the Lord Jesus Christ and by the Spirit of our God" (1 Corinthians 6:11 ESV).

> Don't let the enemy blind you to the truth of
>   who you really are!
> Because you are not who you used to be.
> You are who God says you are.

SCRIPTURE

"Your word is a lamp to guide my feet and a light for my path" (Psalm 119:105 NLT).

—————— *Prayer* ——————

Lord, help me to see the truth of Your character and Your Word clearly. Protect me from the enemy's attempts to blindfold me with deception and despair. Remove the blindfold of shame with the power of Your Holy Spirit in me, reminding me that I am a new creature in Christ. Amen.

> What is impossible for humans is always possible with God! All things are possible when you acknowledge your mess and dare to hope for a miracle.

Just consider how you might feel if you were in the blind man's sandals.

I pray you have 20/20 vision, but just imagine being born into a dark world with no hope of ever seeing the vivid colors, dimensional textures and unique faces all around you. You've missed out on watching the sun fade into gold and pink on the horizon as the first evening stars appear. You've never glimpsed your parents' smiling eyes looking into yours. You've never spied the shimmering colors of a rainbow bridging across the sky after a rainstorm. You don't know what your own arms and legs look like. Only darkness.

Then one day you're sitting by a busy corner, relying on the kindness of those passing by since you're unable to work, when you hear a band of strangers talking and coming toward you. As they draw closer, you overhear them discussing a question you have pondered your entire life: Why were you born blind? Was it something your parents did? Or something you must have done without knowing? Before you can spiral too far into your thoughts, however, one of the men spits on the ground right in front of you. Then He stoops down and touches the ground. Moments later, you realize He's standing in front of you at the same time you feel His fingers gently placing something cool and earthy over your sightless eyes—could that really be *mud* you feel?

Like those watching Jesus administer this most unexpected remedy, you wonder what you're about to experience. But when this Healer instructs you to go to the Pool of Siloam nearby and wash yourself, you don't hesitate. There's something about this situation that sends a tingling current of hope down your spine. You know you're about to change, even if you don't dare imagine that you might finally see. After all, you have never seen—why should you hope for the impossible?

After walking the short distance to Siloam, you begin splashing cool water from the pool onto your mud-caked face. You continue rinsing your face as the dirt trickles away—but suddenly something is different. Your eyelids flutter as your pupils sense light entering them for the first time. As you open your eyes, blurry shapes immediately sharpen into distinct images.

You can see! You can see perfectly all the people lingering near the pool, see the translucence of its waters, the hazy sky above you. You can see every face, shape, color, texture and image before you.

Yes, the technique may seem a little crazy, but the results are undeniable.

What had seemed undeniably impossible only moments ago is now reality. Your unwavering obedience has been rewarded with the gift of sight—something you had never experienced before until that moment. No matter how messy the method, the Messiah makes a miracle!

SCRIPTURE

"Jesus looked at them and said, 'With man this is impossible, but with God all things are possible'" (Matthew 19:26).

— *Prayer* —

Thank You, Lord, that You can do what seems impossible to me! I know that whether I can see evidence of Your miracle in my mess right now or not, You are at work in my life. Give me patience, Father, when Your ways seem unexpected or surprising. Amen.

God is not only the God who restores—He gives you what you've never had before!

Don't be blinded by your past when God wants you focused on your glorious future.

Of all the ways the Lord could have given this blind man his sight, Jesus deliberately made a mess as the precursor to the miracle. Rather than instantly heal the man's eyes and restore his sight, Christ chose a surprising method that emphasizes the messiness that often occurs before the miraculous. Why? Could it be to remind us that nothing is impossible for God? That even the most unlikely, unexpected messes can become fertile soil for harvesting God's power?

Throughout the pages of Scripture, this refrain echoes across the centuries. No matter what you're going through, no matter how dire the circumstances, no matter how unbelievable your loss or unfathomable your pain, you are more than a conqueror through Christ Jesus! What you perceive as impossible is simply an incomplete vision obstructed by your human limitations. When you have the power of the Holy Spirit within you, then you can move mountains with faith as small as a mustard seed (Matthew 17:20).

I'm convinced that God is attracted to impossible circumstances! Show Him your need and get ready for God to show up. Show Him a barren womb, a closed door, a broken heart, a shattered dream, an overdrawn account, a dire diagnosis, a ruined relationship or a dysfunctional family and watch what happens.

I don't care how impossible it looks today—God is about to show up!

He's attracted to the impossible so that no human can get credit for what He's about to do!

Your God is the God of the impossible!

With the woman who had the issue of blood, Jesus gave her back her health.

With the invalid man at Bethesda, He gave him back his walk.

With Lazarus, He gave him back his life.

With another blind man (in Mark 8), He gave him back his sight.

But with this blind man in John 9, Jesus did not give him something he lost.

Jesus gave him something he never had in the first place.

For, you see, there is a difference between God restoring something you had and God giving you something you never had in the first place.

Our God is not only the God who *restores*.

Our God is a God who *gives us what we never had before*.

Our God is Lord of doing what has not been done before! His Word tells us, "Behold, I do a new thing; do you not see it?" (see Isaiah 43:19). Don't focus your time on getting back what you lost when you should be asking God to give you what you've never had in the first place!

God is not interested in renovating your past.

He is more interested in releasing your future.

SCRIPTURE

"Truly I tell you, if you have faith as small as a mustard seed, you can say to this mountain, 'Move from here to there,' and it will move. Nothing will be impossible for you" (Matthew 17:20).

Prayer

Dear God, today I am believing for the impossible! Though my faith feels fragile and small, I know Your power is limitless and Your love is infinite. Thank You for what You're mixing from the mess in my midst. Amen.

> Your mess is the soil for God's miracle. When Christ restores your vision, you will see His power unleashed in your life!

What comes to mind when you think about *messy*?

Beauty may be in the eyes of the beholder—but messy can be just as subjective. What's messy to someone with obsessive-compulsive disorder (OCD) may seem neat and tidy to anyone else. On the other end of the spectrum, you may know some creative types, or consider yourself one, who insist their cluttered desk and disheveled workspace allows them the freedom to innovate and improvise. Or you may know others who border on hoarding anything and everything—food, clothes, papers, appliances and décor items.

When you consider how to define *messy*, you might visualize your garage and the haphazard array of boxes, lawn equipment, gardening tools and Christmas decorations. Perhaps your linen closet comes to mind, jammed full of barely folded towels, sheets, blankets, old comforters and Grandma's quilts. Your idea of messy might simply be your storage space or junk drawer, your cluttered attic or basement playroom.

Messy can also describe more intangible aspects of life—those mental, emotional, relational and contextual areas that seem just as chaotic as any concrete place. Others usually cannot see this kind of messy in your life—at least, not initially. This kind of messy typically dwells in shadows and secrets, in shame and subversion, in deception and duplicity. Messy addictions and messy affairs. Messy finances and messy parenting. Messy rumors and messy manipulations. Messy lies and messy consequences.

More than likely, the longer someone experiences a messy life on the inside, the more their external surroundings reflect their inner turmoil. Many neurologists and psychologists tell us that our brains are wired to organize all the sensory data coming in and make sense of it by ordering it and finding patterns. This not only helps us with drawing conclusions about people but with arranging items in our kitchen.

Similarly, when we live with sinful secrets, habits and relationships that go against what we know is right, what we know God has told us to do, then we experience distress. As the consequences of our choices play out, problems may snowball into an avalanche encompassing most areas of our lives. Soon we lose sight of how things should be in order to protect our secrets, justify our sinful indulgences and hide our mistakes.

This kind of messy can seem harder to clean up than the tangible kind. But the good news is that this type of messy provides the perfect soil for the muddy mixture of miracles only God can bring about. The messy parts of life require supernatural intervention to restore what you've lost and provide what you didn't have before. And nothing is beyond the power of God to heal, transform and redeem!

SCRIPTURE

"I waited patiently for the LORD; he turned to me and heard my cry. He lifted me out of the slimy pit, out of the mud and mire; he set my feet on a rock and gave me a firm place to stand" (Psalm 40:1–2).

Prayer

Father, You know all the messy places in my life and yet You love me still. Thank You for using even the worst things in my life to grow hope and miraculous transformation. Amen.

Jesus meets you in the messy, vulnerable places in your life. He comes to wash away your sins and heal your blindness.

When Jesus healed the man blind since birth, He chose a hands-on, messy method for making this miracle. After Christ spit on the ground, made some mud with the saliva and put it on the man's eyes, He told him to go wash in the Pool of Siloam, and "so the man went and washed, and came home seeing" (John 9:6–7).

While Jesus didn't have to use this messy method, we know nothing is accidental with God, so Jesus definitely had His reasons. Perhaps foremost among them is to illustrate His power to bless our mess into wholeness even when we—like this man blind since birth—cannot see the extent of our messiness. In other words, Jesus heals our vision—our ability to see our sin, our need and God's grace—even when we don't realize just how blind we are!

A similar kind of restoration emerges from another of Christ's most intriguing encounters—with the Samaritan woman at the well. Traveling from Judea to Galilee, Jesus went through Samaria and paused at a spot known as Jacob's well in the town of Sychar (John 4:1–6). A local woman approached the well, intent on filling her water jugs. When Jesus asked her for a drink, she questioned His request because Jews did not usually associate with Samaritans (John 4:9). Jesus responded with a question of His own: "If you knew the gift of God and who it is that asks you for a drink, you would have asked him and he would have given you living water" (John 4:10).

The woman assumed they were still talking literally, not figuratively and spiritually. "Sir, give me this water so that I won't get thirsty and have to keep coming here to draw water" (John 4:15). Jesus then instructed her to fetch her husband and come back, and the woman replied, "I have no husband" (John 4:16–17). Then, in one of the greatest examples of divine revelation, Jesus removed the blindfold from this woman's eyes: "You are right when you say you have no husband. The fact is, you have had five husbands, and the man you now have is not your husband. What you have just said is quite true" (John 4:17–18).

Jesus revealed that He knew all about the messiness in her life.

And He did it with great kindness. He didn't call her a liar or an adulteress or even an immoral woman, but He simply pointed to the truth of her situation, to the factual evidence of the soul thirst she had been trying to quench in ways that never satisfied her longing for more. He didn't confront her right away or call her out on her past behavior. He made it clear that He wasn't there to judge her or to condemn her—He was there to heal her.

He was there to bless her mess.

Just like He wants to bless yours!

SCRIPTURE

"Heal me, LORD, and I will be healed; save me and I will be saved, for you are the one I praise" (Jeremiah 17:14).

—————————— *Prayer* ——————————

Thank You, Lord, for knowing all the places in my life that are messy and shameful and loving me too much to leave me there. Remind me that You are meeting me in the messiness in order to produce Your miracle. Amen.

Jesus helps you see yourself as He sees you—not as the person you used to be, but as the child of God you are now!

During His encounter with the Samaritan woman at the well, Jesus waited to confirm His identity until she arrived at the truth. Rather than announce that He was the Messiah when they first met, Christ demonstrated His ability to see her and her need for living water. Jesus helped her see what she could not see in herself—and to see it in a way resulting in grace and not shame (John 4:25–30).

The woman then became so excited about meeting Jesus that she left her water jar at the well! Most likely, this had never happened before. Basically, she went there on a mundane errand in the middle of the day and left transformed by her encounter with the Messiah, the Giver of living water. Her testimony must have made quite an impression, too, because many of her neighbors from town also believed in Christ.

No longer would she be known as a woman with multiple relationships and a shady past.

Now she was an evangelist for the Messiah, who had changed her life.

When you encounter Jesus and drink the living water only He gives, when you experience the ability to see clearly, then your life will never be the same. He is not put off by your mess, by your past, or by your inability to see yourself clearly. Jesus told His followers, "I have come that they may have life, and have it to the full" (John 10:10). And His gift of new life remains the same for us today.

The Samaritan woman could never have expected or even imagined that she would encounter the Messiah, the long-awaited Son of God the prophets had been describing for the past four hundred years, on an average day doing an average chore. She had no idea that morning that her priorities were about to shift and her relationships were about to change. She didn't realize walking along the hot, dusty path to Jacob's well that she was about to encounter the living God. She couldn't see then what she could see after meeting Him.

Never underestimate the impact your mess-turned-miracle can have on other people. Remember that Jesus told His disciples that the blind man's limitation was not the result of his sin or the sin of his parents, but rather an opportunity for God's glory to be manifest. The same is true for whatever mess you may be mired in right now. God uses our messes to get our attention as well as the attention of others. Just as we're inspired by the examples of the blind man and the Samaritan woman, other people will soon be inspired by our story as well!

SCRIPTURE

"God is our refuge and strength, an ever-present help in trouble. Therefore we will not fear, though the earth give way and the mountains fall into the heart of the sea" (Psalm 46:1–2).

Prayer

Jesus, You have changed my life forever, and I am no longer who I used to be. No matter how messy my life may seem, I know Your Spirit will sustain me. Amen.

When you walk by faith in the power of the Holy Spirit, you must be prepared to receive your miracle when you least expect it.

Sometimes the least likely, messiest moments become the most unexpected, miraculous ones. The blind man didn't realize he was about to receive the gift of sight from the One who created him. He had no idea that gooey mud held together by the Master's spit would give him what he had never had before. The blind man experienced the power of Jesus through a dirty, messy mask of miraculous mud.

The Samaritan woman at the well that day didn't expect to see her messy life washed clean by the Messiah. She didn't anticipate that a stranger could see her heart and know all about her life. She didn't dare hope that a drink of well water might lead to a soul-quenching spring of eternal life.

You may not be expecting to see what God's about to do next in your life, but that doesn't mean you shouldn't be ready. In fact, based on the way Jesus poured His power into those He healed and encountered, you should expect to be surprised! In Jesus' name, you are about to see what you have never seen before.

You're about to see the power of Jesus heal, transform, illuminate, save, sanctify and elevate in ways you have never witnessed. Powered by the Holy Spirit, you are about to see God work in ways that leave your eyes wide, your mouth open, your spine tingling and your heart singing. You are about to see your marriage healed, your abilities transformed and your health touched by the Great Physician.

Just because you cannot imagine your miracle, it doesn't mean that God's power is not already rooted in the midst of your mud. Just because there's mud in your eyes right now, it doesn't mean you're not about to receive new vision. Just because your soul remains thirsty right now, it doesn't mean you're not about to be quenched with the satisfaction of living water.

Don't worry if you feel skeptical or have your doubts. You may have been waiting a long time already for God to unleash His miraculous power and healing touch in your life. You may have been praying and obeying, seeking and knocking for weeks, months or years up until now. But this only means you're closer to your breakthrough than you've ever been before!

So, no matter how hard you've been hit by COVID or cancer or diabetes or depression or anxiety, your miracle is waiting. No matter how much debt, how many divorces or how little money you have in the bank. No matter how dirty, sordid, shameful and muddy your mess may be, it is about to become God's miracle!

Your worst mess is about to become your best miracle!

SCRIPTURE

"But, as it is written, 'What no eye has seen, nor ear heard, nor the heart of man imagined, what God has prepared for those who love him'" (1 Corinthians 2:9 ESV).

Prayer

Dear Lord, help me to see ways I can prepare to receive the miracle You have for me. Give me patience and peace as I persevere through the messy times in order to experience the miraculous times ahead. Amen.

When darkness closes in around you and obscures your vision, don't lose hope. Sometimes your mess gets messier just before God's miracle restores the light and heals your sight!

If the old saying is true, that it's darkest before the dawn, then it's also no surprise everything seems messiest before it's most miraculous.

When life gets messy, though, the darkness can dim your vision. As a culture, a nation and a world, we have all seen darkness cast shade on our hopes and dreams. We have seen the shadows fall over the ruins of what once was. The ruins of racial and social unrest destroying property, fragmenting families, dividing communities and shattering the Church. The ruins of political unrest where the donkey and the elephant temporarily succeed in dividing what belongs to the Lamb.

The ruins of a life you struggle to enjoy because you're so overwhelmed by the pressing demands pulling you in every direction.

The ruins of dreams you once pursued with energy and excitement, only to watch them dwindle to cold ashes of disappointment and regret.

The ruins of hope that once sustained your ability to see the light despite the shadows gathering around you on every side.

But God can use those ruins to create a miracle masterpiece. Broken pieces cannot be put back together, but they can be used to build something more beautiful, more significant, more holy. No matter how bleak your situation, no matter how harsh your circumstances, no matter how desperate you may feel—do not lose hope! Because your tears are not in vain. God's Word promises: "Weeping may tarry for the night, but joy comes with the morning" (Psalm 30:5 ESV). No matter how long your night seems, your joy is coming!

A new day is dawning.

Night is coming to an end.

You may be in the dark right now, but new light glimmers ahead!

No matter what your mess looks like, no matter how much damage it has done in your life and the lives of those you love, no matter how desperate you may feel, open your eyes to the power of Jesus Christ in your life. Invite Him in to play in the mud at your feet. Meet Him at the old well and let Him see you right where you are. Ask the Holy Spirit to give you eyes to see what you have never seen before! Expect the unexpected and anticipate a fresh encounter with your Savior.

It may be darkest before the dawn, but the light always dawns.

And as the light of a new day, a new season, shines around you, you will see what you have never seen before. You will glimpse God's miracle emerging from what was once your mess. You will gaze and be amazed as God exceeds anything you could have imagined.

Look with wonder as the power of Christ radically transforms your life!

SCRIPTURE

"Wait for the LORD; be strong and take heart and wait for the LORD" (Psalm 27:14).

—————————— *Prayer* ——————————

God, You know how difficult it is for me to see in the darkness. During those moments, assure me of Your presence and Your purpose for my life. Give me strength to trust You and to take the next step. Amen.

What if you've been waiting on God's miracle when God's waiting on you to step forward in faith to receive it?

What if what you've been looking for is right in front of you?

Like most of us, you've probably had times when you couldn't find your keys, phone, sunglasses or wallet. You know you just had it a few minutes ago when it suddenly seems to have disappeared. With so many responsibilities, demands and interruptions during your day, you know you could have left the lost item in a number of places. Then you realize it's right in front of you—on your desk, beside the vase, in your pocket or hanging by the front door.

Similarly, we often lose sight of what God is doing in our lives because we're looking everywhere except right in our midst.

We miss out on seeing what we have in the present because we're stuck in the past and unable to imagine moving forward again. We lose sight of how God is providing and leading and sustaining even during times when we feel lost in the dark. Other times, we're living conditionally in the future. We assume we'll have more power, more peace, more joy and purpose someday when we're more spiritually mature.

But often we're waiting on God to move in our lives, to answer our prayers or to reveal our next steps, when God is waiting on us to see what's right in front of us! We're waiting on God for our miracle when He's already started shaping it from our mess. When we're willing to open our eyes spiritually, we see God has already given us all we need and more.

Sometimes we fail to see what God is doing in our lives because we rely on what others think of us. Even when they realize there's something different about us due to God's presence, we may try to convince them that we're just like them, the same person we've always been.

After Jesus healed the man who had been blind since birth, others didn't recognize him. They knew he resembled the blind beggar they were accustomed to seeing most days—only this man could see! When this man told those around him that he had indeed been blind until moments ago, they wanted to know what happened, of course. So, he told them how Jesus had made mud, coated his eyes and told him to wash (John 9:8–12).

The man's neighbors likely couldn't fathom how someone they knew a particular way could be transformed so dramatically. Perhaps the man himself was still stunned by the miracle that had just occurred in his life. Because the miraculous power of God's Spirit changes everything—including how you see yourself, see others and see God!

> *Whether you can see it happening or not,*
> *God's miracle is emerging from your mess.*

SCRIPTURE

"And we know that in all things God works for the good of those who love him, who have been called according to his purpose" (Romans 8:28).

--- *Prayer* ---

Dear Lord, I know Your ways are higher than mine even as I am limited by my human senses. Strengthen my faith when I cannot see what You're doing in front of me. May I continue to trust You are at work in my life, shaping the messy pieces of my brokenness into Your masterpiece. Amen.

day

12

When you experience God's miracle amid your messes, your perspective changes! Everything looks different because you are different.

The previously blind man's neighbors tried to talk themselves out of the truth of what they saw by assuming it was just coincidental resemblance. They had grown accustomed to perceiving and identifying this man based only on his lack of sight. Perhaps he usually sat and begged at a certain location near the Temple, and that's the only context they had for who he was and what he was about. He was simply the blind man who begged, someone they pitied but dismissed as irrelevant to their lives.

Sometimes you may become so familiar with someone, including yourself, in a certain location and context that you lose the ability to recognize them any
other way. They become part of the landscape or a
player in a certain role during your day—the barista at
your coffee shop, the homeless person on the corner,
the clerk in the convenience store, the receptionist
at your doctor's office. With repeated viewings over
time, they are seen and identified only by association
with what they do in a particular locale at a particular
time. For those passing them every day, their identity
doesn't exist outside that time and place.

Until something changes and you're forced to see
others in a different light.

After you encounter the sight-giving, life-changing,
heart-transforming power of Jesus, you no longer see
things the same way because you are no longer who
you once were. Once you were blind, but now you
can see. Once you were lost, but now you are found.
Once you despaired at life's messes; now you await
God's miracles.

When this shift occurs in you, others may not recognize you because your attitude, speech and behavior
changes, sometimes dramatically. The thoughts and

activities that once held your attention no longer matter when your focus shifts to knowing God and living by His Spirit. The darkness that once seemed familiar, perhaps even comfortable, can no longer obscure your vision. Everything looks different because you are different!

Once you give your life to Christ and the Holy Spirit dwells in you, you see things differently. Old pursuits and idolatrous habits lose their power over you. You realize that some relationships that once sustained you were actually holding you back. Your eyes become focused on an eternal perspective that glorifies God and advances His Kingdom. You recognize spiritual movement in others and glimpse the Holy Spirit at work in ways you did not notice previously.

Because seeing is about much more than what's before your eyes.

Who you are is much more than the roles you play.

Once you experience miraculous power in your messes, you are never the same.

SCRIPTURE

"Therefore, if anyone is in Christ, he is a new creation; old things have passed away; behold, all things have become new" (2 Corinthians 5:17 NKJV).

—————————— *Prayer* ——————————

Lord, grant me peace, purpose and power as I learn to see with spiritual clarity. Remind me of my true identity when others question the changes they're noticing in my life. Help me to trust You during those times when I don't recognize myself! Amen.

day

13

As you experience God's miracle in your mess, it can take time to shift your vision to an eternal perspective. Be patient as your eyes adjust to the reality of living in God's light!

The healing of the man blind since birth is not the only time Jesus restored the vision of someone who failed to see clearly. One of the best and most dramatic examples of a before-and-after transformation in the Bible occurred in the life of the apostle Paul. Previously known as Saul, he not only didn't know Christ—he actively persecuted followers of Jesus, determined to use violence or whatever means necessary to prevent them from spreading the Gospel. Saul had been raised in a strict household that conditioned him in the rigid legalism of Jewish religious practices.

Based on his allegiance to traditional Judaism, Saul apparently considered Jesus to be a dangerous heretic, and His followers just as harmful to the Jewish faith. Then one day while traveling to Damascus in hopes of capturing and arresting more followers of the Way, Saul was literally stopped in his tracks as a heavenly light flashed around him. Blinded, he fell to the ground as a voice asked him, "Saul, Saul, why do you persecute me?" (Acts 9:4). When Saul asked the identity of the unseen speaker, the voice replied, "I am Jesus, whom you are persecuting. Now get up and go into the city, and you will be told what you must do" (Acts 9:5–6).

While Saul physically could see, he failed to realize the truth that Jesus was the Messiah, the Son of God come to earth in human form. How ironic then that Saul's encounter with Christ leaves the bounty hunter blind, which finally parallels the spiritual state in which he had been living. Saul's blindness also forced him to come to terms with what he had been missing. Notice that Jesus asks him, "Why are you persecuting Me?" Implicit in this question is another, more personal one: "Why can't you see who I am? Why are you blind to the truth?"

It's the same question Jesus continues to ask us today—even after we've invited Him into our lives. Sometimes when we live in shadows, we're initially blinded by the power of God's Light. Just as our eyes adjust while our pupils constrict in bright light, we discover we must adjust our vision spiritually.

Without a doubt, at least from a spiritual perspective, Saul's life was a mess. He not only failed to see the truth of Christ in his own life, but he was committed to eradicating this truth in the lives of others. Basically, Saul worked for the enemy by persecuting believers and trying to prevent the good news of the Gospel from spreading. But where Saul thought he was going was not where the apostle we know as Paul ended up going!

When you experience God's miracle in your mess, you surrender your previous priorities in order to serve the Lord and advance His Kingdom. What you failed to see before now becomes crystal clear with your advanced spiritual vision. Don't be afraid to see what you've been missing!

SCRIPTURE

"For if, while we were God's enemies, we were reconciled to him through the death of his Son, how much more, having been reconciled, shall we be saved through his life!" (Romans 5:10).

—————————— *Prayer* ——————————

Jesus, thank You for intervening when I am not seeing what You want me to see. Give me new eyes so that I may focus on what matters most to You. Help me see others with compassion, love and mercy. Amen.

Our God is not only the God of messy miracles. Our God redirects our purpose and satisfies our deepest longings!

If someone had told Saul, the Jewish zealot who lived to persecute Christians, the incredible impact he would have for spreading the Gospel of Jesus Christ, he would never have believed them. But such is the power of God in our lives to do what we ourselves could never do on our own. So often we think we know what we're doing and how we'll do it. We rely on human logic and probability, interpreting our perceptions to see only what we want to see while remaining blind to the power of God's truth in our lives.

When we're filled with the Spirit, we surrender our own agendas, schedules and itineraries in order to go where He directs when He wants us to go. Many times, when we allow the Spirit to guide us, we find ourselves outside our comfort zones and inside God's incredible plan for our lives. While we usually want to know where we're going and what to expect, the reality is that God's plan transcends the route we would choose.

On the other hand, when we become blinded to the power of God within us, we often look for fulfillment elsewhere, usually in some sinful pursuit or idol. Saul believed that by following the Law of Moses according to Jewish traditions, he was a righteous man. Those who refused to follow these laws and customs because of the freedom they found in Jesus clearly enraged Saul. He had to encounter Christ and experience physical blindness in order to overcome the spiritual blindness that was his central problem.

Although most of us don't lose our physical vision when our spiritual vision is obscured, we nonetheless experience blindness. Perhaps we fail to see the truth about a relationship that's harming us and convince ourselves to remain in a dangerous situation. It might be going deeper in debt rather than seeing the harsh truth about the state of our finances. We might be in denial about our physical health or the impact of a lingering trauma in our lives. We see what we want to see and refuse to see the truth of our situation, factually as well as spiritually.

Often when we're blinding ourselves to the truth, we fixate on something we believe will fulfill us. If this relationship didn't work out, maybe the next one will. If the problem is spending, then more money is bound to help. If our body causes us pain, then medication or alcohol can dull our senses and lessen our suffering. Eventually, however, we realize we can only ignore what we've refused to see for so long. Then the truth, one way or another, opens our eyes to what we've been missing.

SCRIPTURE

"If you hold to my teaching, you are really my disciples. Then you will know the truth, and the truth will set you free" (John 8:31–32).

—————————— *Prayer* ——————————

Father God, forgive me for the times I have remained blind by chasing sinful pleasures and pursuing prideful achievements through my own power. Allow me to see clearly Your glorious plan for my life and to rely only on the power of Your Holy Spirit. Amen.

Seeing clearly with the eyes of your heart requires you to focus on the only source of lasting satisfaction—the love of your heavenly Father, the sacrifice of His Son, and the gift of His Holy Spirit.

In the parable of the prodigal son (Luke 15:11–24), Jesus illustrated the acute blindness we suffer when we look elsewhere for our identity, purpose and fulfillment in life. Christ described a man with two sons, and the younger son grew so restless that he did the unthinkable by demanding his inheritance right away. So, the father relented and divided his property between his two sons (Luke 15:12).

The younger son immediately left home in pursuit of his heart's desire, squandering his newfound wealth in wild living. About the time his money ran out, a severe famine forced him to work—feeding pigs. To add insult to injury, his hunger was such that he would have gladly eaten the pigs' food (Luke 15:13–16).

Alone at the pig trough, the younger son could no longer sustain his blindness and regretted his foolish choices. There was no one to blame but himself, and facing the stark truth required experiencing the pain, regret and loneliness of his dire situation. But even in the midst of such emotional, physical and spiritual turmoil, the young man saw something else that was unmistakably true—he had a choice to remain blinded or to return to his father and regain his sight.

Like he was waking from a bad dream, the young man gained crystal clarity of himself and his situation in a moment of epiphany. Coming to his senses, he realized that even the hired servants back at his father's house never went hungry. As humbling, even humiliating, as it would be to return home, he chose to ask for his father's forgiveness in hopes of being treated like the lowliest of servants (Luke 15:17–20).

Are there areas of your life in which you need to come to your senses?

When you're challenged by a tough day, how do you respond?

Do you demand your inheritance right away and feel entitled to find relief through a harmful habit, old addiction or temporary pleasure?

Do you prop up the image of yourself you want others to see on social media rather than the flawed, needy person you are in that moment?

Do you envy what others have and assume their happiness can only be found in your own pursuits?

These are not easy questions to answer, but they can help you open your eyes to the truth of what you've been missing. It's time to see what God wants to do in your life! Whether you've strayed from God and know it's time to come home, or you've been blinded by the distractions and demands of looking elsewhere, it's time to open your eyes and see clearly.

SCRIPTURE

"But while he was still a long way off, his father saw him and was filled with compassion for him; he ran to his son, threw his arms around him and kissed him" (Luke 15:20).

Prayer

Heavenly Father, thank You for being a God who runs toward me when I become blinded by the things of this world and distracted by the temptations around me. Please forgive me for seeking life in anything but You. Through the power of Jesus and the guidance of the Holy Spirit, I know that I can see. Amen.

day

16

Do not mistake your dirty process for God's cleansing promise. You don't have Christ's spit—you have His Spirit!

When you consider the study of DNA, you probably think about your biology and science classes before you consider one of Jesus' messiest miracles. But the way Jesus chose to heal the man blind from birth was not only unexpected—it was intimate and incarnational. Because Christ did not simply lay hands on the blind man or heal from a distance. No, the Son of God connected His humanity to the man's calamity.

Jesus transferred something inside Himself to heal someone with an external need obvious to everyone around him: "Then he spit on the ground, made mud with the saliva, and spread the mud over the blind man's eyes" (John 9:6 NLT). Christ didn't simply choose to heal this man—He literally gave the blind man part of Himself so the man might receive something he had lacked since birth. Jesus gave this man His divine DNA!

While the disciples might not have been surprised that their Master chose to heal this blind man, they were most likely startled by His method. Spitting, the act of expelling saliva or something from one's mouth, was an act, then as now, that you simply didn't do in public. Not only spitting on the ground, Jesus used His saliva to make mud that He then caked over the blind man's non-functioning eyes. The method was messy, dirty, grimy, grubby, earthy.

But there is no better metaphor for the way Jesus continues to restore our sight today! The unorthodox method He used to facilitate a miracle reflects His willingness to enter the messiness, the murkiness and the muddiness of our lives. Sometimes the process requires getting down in the mud. Sometimes the process is complicated. Sometimes we get dirty from living life before we get clean from the Giver of eternal life.

Even after we come to know the Lord, we can fall back into old habits and thought patterns. Whether it's gossiping about those we dislike at work, cheating on our expense reports, lying to our loved ones, idolizing social media or giving in to illicit behavior, we know we're not doing what God wants us to do. Instead of living by His guidelines and the power of His Holy Spirit, we try to go our own way. We lose sight of what matters most. We hide from the glare of God's light. We resign ourselves to sinful struggles in the shadows. We get stuck in the grime and assume God can't meet us in our mud-stained, tear-soaked, spit-stirred circumstances.

But that is simply not true.

Jesus chose a method to heal the blind man that applies to us today.

Thanks be to God that we have a Savior who's never been afraid to get dirty!

SCRIPTURE

"Oh, what a miserable person I am! Who will free me from this life that is dominated by sin and death? Thank God! The answer is in Jesus Christ our Lord" (Romans 7:24–25 NLT).

--- *Prayer* ---

Thank You, Lord, for the ways You remind me of Your understanding, acceptance and love. Your humanity shows me the way You have bridged heaven and earth through Your death on the cross. Your deity reveals the way I can know You and experience eternal life. Amen.

day

17

Jesus made it clear that He came to meet our needs in the messiness of life. Knowing you need what only Christ can provide dispels your blindness!

With His muddy method for healing the blind man, Jesus was not only unconcerned with getting dirty, literally, but He was also known for engaging people with messy lives. After Jesus invited Matthew, a tax collector, to follow Him, the gospel account written by Matthew himself reveals, "While Jesus was having dinner at Matthew's house, many tax collectors and sinners came and ate with him and his disciples" (Matthew 9:10).

Keep in mind that tax collectors at that time were considered dishonest, greedy and unscrupulous, willing to cheat both the citizens they taxed and the government officials they paid. No wonder then that the Jewish religious leaders took notice and inquired about why the self-proclaimed Messiah would associate with such undesirables. Jesus answered them by explaining, "It is not the healthy who need a doctor, but the sick. . . . I have not come to call the righteous, but sinners" (Matthew 9:12–13).

His response to them resonates with the same answer He gave to His disciples when they saw the blind man and asked, "Rabbi, who sinned, this man or his parents, that he was born blind?" (John 9:2). In the Jewish world of the Law, most matters of sin were identified by external appearances and behaviors rather than thoughts in the mind and attitudes in the heart. This system conditioned religious leaders to focus only on their public behavior, not their private words and deeds.

This interior spiritual focus also explains why Jesus repeatedly rebuked the Pharisees and Sadducees for their hypocrisy, comparing their double standard to a dirty dish: "Woe to you, teachers of the law and Pharisees, you hypocrites! You clean the outside of the cup and dish, but inside they are full of greed and self-indulgence. Blind Pharisee! First clean the inside of the cup and dish, and then the outside also will be clean" (Matthew 23:25–26).

Jesus made it clear that we must begin from the inside out, with our hearts. Going through the motions of righteous behavior, as difficult as it may be, will always be easier than confessing the truth of our sinful hearts before God and others and receiving forgiveness and mercy.

Jesus is the only way we can cleanse our hearts and follow through with our actions. Which brings us back to His answer to the disciples' question about a causal correlation between sin and the blind man's condition. Jesus explained, "Neither this man nor his parents sinned, but this happened so that the works of God might be displayed in him" (John 9:3).

Jesus Christ shines with God's grace for the glory of His Father.

His grace is already shining through you, no matter how messy your life might be.

SCRIPTURE

"For the LORD sees not as man sees: man looks on the outward appearance, but the LORD looks on the heart" (1 Samuel 16:7 ESV).

Prayer

Dear God, I am so grateful that You remain willing to meet me in the messes of life. Because no matter how hard I try, I can never live up to Your standard of holiness based on my own abilities. Your Holy Spirit empowers me to do what I can't accomplish on my own, revealing Your glory in the process. Amen.

day

18

Don't lose sight of God's promise in the midst of the messiness of His method. Where you are right now is not where you will be as He restores your sight and empowers your life!

When Jesus used His holy spit, His divine DNA, to make mud for a miracle, He reminded us to focus on the perfection of His promise, not the messiness in the method. Because the process is temporary while the promise is permanent! We often get so blinded by our pain, disappointment, anger and grief, we overlook that the God of the outcome is the same God of the process. Unable to see clearly, we start to confuse what we're going through with where we're going to.

There's no doubt that life can be brutally hard at times. Our world often seems to have spun off its axis, leaving collateral damage of pandemics and pandemonium left and right. Interest rates go up, gas prices go up, grocery prices go up while our paycheck does well to stay the same. Family and friends struggle with loss, addiction, depression and despair, and their struggles hurt our hearts. Adult children stray from home and turn from the Lord, and our pain multiplies. Worry, anxiety and uncertainty often take turns overwhelming us on an hourly basis.

But no matter what you're going through, you must remember this: Your temporary has run its course while your permanent is just getting started. Because if you're going through what you've never experienced before, then it's only because you're about to step into what you've never stepped into before!

Just as the blind man discovered that day, your DNA is not the same as Christ's DNA.

When Jesus transferred His DNA to the blind man's eyes, He revealed a study in contrasts for what we can't see now but will see through the eyes of our hearts by the power of His Spirit. If we want to see spiritually, then we must be willing to open our eyes by faith, even when there's mud from our past obscuring our vision. God's Word tells us, "Now faith is confidence in what we hope for and assurance about what we do not see" (Hebrews 11:1).

God has given you the gift of His Holy Spirit in order that you might see what you've never seen before. To do what you cannot do on your own. To become who He made you to be.

In other words, with your DNA you cannot see beyond the tangible and temporal.

But with His DNA you can see the spiritual and eternal!

With your DNA you are a victim.

With His DNA you are more than a conqueror!

With your DNA you are limited.

With His DNA you can do all things through Christ, who gives you strength!

With your DNA you will make excuses.

But with His DNA you will make history!

What Christ gave you wasn't His spit, but His Spirit!

SCRIPTURE

"Now all glory to God, who is able, through his mighty power at work within us, to accomplish infinitely more than we might ask or think" (Ephesians 3:20 NLT).

——————————— *Prayer* ———————————

Lord and Savior, Your healing power is transforming me in ways I can't even imagine. The same resurrection power that overcame Your death now dwells in me through Your Holy Spirit. Thank You for shining Your glory through the broken, messy places in my life. Amen.

Sometimes you're waiting for God to produce a miracle when He's waiting on you to realize what He's already doing! Don't overlook the power of God's Spirit right where you are.

Too often, we're tempted to focus on dates, dimensions and details when God wants to give us more power, purpose and peace. We're hung up on the "when," and He's intent on giving us the "how." We can't see a way forward, and so we want the Lord to connect all the dots for us. "I know You're going to help me get through this trial, Lord," we say, "but what's that going to look like and when will it end? Could You please give me the time and date?"

But here's the problem. When you get hung up about the details of what God's doing in your life, you may miss out on the delivery. When you're focused only on how messy your process seems, you may miss out on the miracle of His promise. When you're blinded by the temporary obstacles of the present, you might miss out on the eternal perspective of your future.

If we think we need to understand how the miracle works before we receive it, then we're getting in the way of what God wants to give us. Our brains are wonderful organs in our bodies. Our intellects are gifts that help us reason, think, remember, analyze, create and choose. But our minds can get in the way of receiving God's Spirit if we let our rational, logical ways guard the gates of our hearts. It's one thing to know about God as you expect His miracle in your mess. It's another thing to experience His power right in the middle of your mess!

Just imagine if the man blind from birth had limited the miracle of his own healing by focusing on the method Jesus chose. "Lord, did You just spit on the ground? Gross! And now You're touching my eyes with that? Really? Why? What's going on?" As comical as such a near-sighted response might be, we basically do the same when we resist God's power in the midst of our messiness. We assume there's no way He could use our mistakes, our weaknesses, our failures in order to accomplish His purposes. We expect earthly details, and God gives us heavenly power.

How often are you missing opportunities to receive all the resources of the Holy Spirit because you don't think it feels the way you expected?

Have you been waiting on God to grant you what you're asking while He's waiting on you to realize you already have access to the power of His Spirit?

Don't overlook the miracle taking place in your life right now through methods that may seem messy.

SCRIPTURE

"But you will receive power when the Holy Spirit comes on you; and you will be my witnesses in Jerusalem, and in all Judea and Samaria, and to the ends of the earth" (Acts 1:8).

Prayer

Lord, forgive me for those times I'm waiting on You and failing to see You have already given me all I need. Thank You for the power of the Holy Spirit dwelling inside me. Open my eyes so I can glimpse Your miracle through the muddy mess around me. Amen.

Everything changes when you have the gift of the Holy Spirit in your life. Your messy parts and soiled struggles become the fertile ground for God's miracles!

When the gift of the Holy Spirit arrived, the impact was unmistakable. The followers of Jesus had gathered together on the Day of Pentecost when they heard a violent wind blowing over them and saw tongues of fire descend on each person. They began to speak in other languages as the Spirit enabled them (Acts 2:1–4). Filled with God's Spirit, Peter preached, and about three thousand people accepted the message of the Gospel (Acts 2:41).

We have many other examples of the Holy Spirit at work in the early Church. And the power those followers of Jesus received is the same power we receive when we accept God's gift of salvation through Jesus and invite the Spirit to dwell in our hearts. The Bible promises, "The Spirit of God, who raised Jesus from the dead, lives in you. And just as God raised Christ Jesus from the dead, he will give life to your mortal bodies by this same Spirit living within you" (Romans 8:11 NLT).

If you have accepted the free gift of salvation through God's grace, then you have the resurrection power of Jesus Christ dwelling in you! The same kind of death-conquering power God used to raise His Son from the dead! Through the power of the Holy Spirit, there's nothing you can't accomplish for God's glory. You simply have to allow the mud to fall away so you can see clearly. You only have to step out in faith and discover all that God has for you.

Once God's Spirit has come into our lives, we are never alone. He guides us, knows us, comforts us and reveals to us. He empowers us and enlightens us. He restores our sight when we're temporarily blinded by circumstances, emotions or temptations. The Holy Spirit does all these things and so much more.

The Holy Spirit is not a denomination, network, emotion or experience.

The Holy Spirit is not a service, conference, event or instruction.

The Holy Spirit is not an ideology, philosophy, theology or technology.

The Holy Spirit is simply the most powerful Person and Force on planet earth today!

This is the same limitless power dwelling in you.

No matter how dirty, muddy or grimy you think your situation has become, if you've been washed in the blood of the Lamb, then you can be whiter than snow. You may have messed up, given in, fallen down, tripped over, stumbled in and stayed down more times than you can count. But you will always rise again by the resurrection power infusing every ounce of your being.

Your miracle is inevitable when your method relies on the power of the Holy Spirit!

SCRIPTURE

"I will ask the Father, and he will give you another Advocate, who will never leave you. He is the Holy Spirit, who leads into all truth" (John 14:16–17 NLT).

Prayer

Dear God, thank You for the gift of Your Holy Spirit dwelling in me. Help me to see with the eyes of my heart all You want to show me. Never let me forget that I can do all things through the power of Your Spirit in me. Amen.

day
21

God meets us with incarnational power in the form of Jesus, fully human and fully God. Experiencing His incarnational power is essential if we want to grow in our faith.

All mud is not the same. Its quality and consistency rely on the ratio of dirt to liquid as well as other environmental factors, particularly temperature and rainfall. The quality and amount of ingredients—particularly phosphorous, potassium and nitrogen—make a big difference as well. Certainly, the mud Jesus created with His own spit and the dust at His feet was one of a kind!

The muddy mask placed over the blind man's sightless eyes not only contained divine DNA, but it included the dirt of His homeland. Jesus chose to use what was already present to produce a miracle unlike

93

any other. Heaven and earth met as Jesus infused the dusty ground with His divine power.

This unique combination recalls the way God created man to begin with: "Then the LORD God formed a man from the dust of the ground and breathed into his nostrils the breath of life, and the man became a living being" (Genesis 2:7). Instead of saliva, God breathed the breath of life into the man He formed from the dust of the ground, which He created in His own image (Genesis 1:27). Just like Jesus with the blind man, God the Father instilled life into dust to create something new.

The miraculous mud Jesus made also symbolizes who He was, both God and man, when living in this world. The Bible tells us that the Son of God was fully human while also fully, perfectly divine—which enabled Him to atone for our sins once and for all, paying the debt we could not pay. "For this reason he had to be made like them, fully human in every way, in order that he might become a merciful and faithful high priest in service to God, and that he might make atonement for the sins of the people. Because he himself suffered when he was tempted, he is able to help those who are being tempted" (Hebrews 2:17–18).

By choosing to add His supernatural saliva to the dusty ground below, Jesus illustrated how He bridges heaven and earth, enabling all of us not only to see spiritually but to experience relationship with God our Father. We have access to this same incarnational power when we invite the Holy Spirit to dwell in us.

Sometimes, though, we don't follow through on obeying God's commands and instructions. Our faith remains weak and immature while our commitment to God stays half-hearted. We don't experience God's power and presence fully unleashed in our lives. We don't produce healthy spiritual fruit that fulfills our true potential.

Why? Because we don't provide fertile soil.

In order to experience God's miracle in our mess, we must do our part.

SCRIPTURE

"The Word became flesh and made his dwelling among us. We have seen his glory, the glory of the one and only Son, who came from the Father, full of grace and truth" (John 1:14).

Prayer

Lord, help me to see the areas of my life where I have failed to surrender to You and Your miraculous power. Give me strength and wisdom to do my part in providing fertile spiritual soil so that I may produce the fruits of the Spirit. Amen.

In order to see clearly and to experience God's miraculous power in your life, you must rely on His Spirit to keep you nourished and anchored.

Your power source determines your growth rate.

On any given day, on what do you rely to accomplish what's before you? How often do you allow God's Spirit to empower you and guide you? While you may want to trust God and walk by faith each day, many people don't experience this because they're not growing and maturing in their faith. And they're not growing and maturing in their faith because they're trying to live in their own strength and abilities. They're attempting to produce supernatural results through natural methods!

When we accept the free gift of salvation through Jesus Christ and welcome the indwelling of His Spirit, we experience what Jesus described as being "born again" (John 3:3), because just as our bodies were born from flesh, "the Spirit gives birth to spirit" (John 3:6). And what exactly does this mean? "This means that anyone who belongs to Christ has become a new person. The old life is gone; a new life has begun!" (2 Corinthians 5:17 NLT).

This new life we have comes from Christ through the power of His Spirit in us. He is the Vine, and we are the branches, dependent on Him for sustained strength, nourishment, power and fruitfulness (John 15:5–8). We only experience true spiritual growth by remaining in Christ's power and obeying His commands. When we go our own way and choose not to remain in Christ, then we wither and die. When His words take root in our hearts, however, then we have full access to the limitless, infinite power of almighty God.

Almost anything that grows also needs light, including your spirit as you walk by faith in God's light. "For you were once darkness, but now you are light in the Lord. Live as children of light" (Ephesians 5:8). Once you begin growing and maturing in your faith, then you begin to glimpse the new life God has for you. Your new life in Christ allows God to fulfill all He has created you to be.

When you live in the power of the Spirit, you experience God's best for your life. No matter what has happened in your life, God can use the dirty, muddy, gritty parts if you're willing to surrender them to Him. He can use the unlikeliest methods to produce the most unimaginable miracles. Once you have been born again, you have new life through the Vine.

You are no longer what you once were.

You are a new creature in Christ, my friend!

You are no longer who you once were.

You are the son or daughter of the King of kings!

SCRIPTURE

"'For I know the plans I have for you,' says the LORD. 'They are plans for good and not for disaster, to give you a future and a hope'" (Jeremiah 29:11 NLT).

Prayer

Lord, give me patience to trust that I am growing stronger in my faith and closer to You every day. Remind me that I belong to You and that I am no longer trapped in the muddy pits of my own desperate efforts. Help me to rely solely on the power of Your Spirit today. Amen.

Growing in Christ requires planting God's Word into the soil of our lives and cultivating its truth in our messes.

How we cultivate, fertilize, nurture, protect and grow the power of the living Word in us makes all the difference. In fact, Jesus told a parable about the results of planting seeds on various kinds of soils that illustrates this truth (Mark 4:3–9). Farmers, those who speak the truth of the Gospel, sow the Word to those who hear them preach and teach. Whether the Word takes root so that they grow spiritually depends on the quality of the soil and how each person responds to adverse conditions.

Some people are like shallow soil along the path; they're robbed by the enemy before the seed can take root. Apparently, they hear the Word, but they don't know how to cultivate it in the midst of assaults from the devil. They have no spiritual armor or connection to God's power to win these battles. They get stuck in the mud permanently.

Next comes rocky soil. These people receive the Word with joy, but they don't allow it to sink into a deeper level where it can take root—apparently because they don't have a deeper level. Trials, adversity and persecution kill the seed in them because the Word is not rooted deeply enough. Perhaps they are unwilling to trust God beyond their circumstances. Perhaps they don't realize the power inside the seed.

Thorny ground proves just as hazardous. These people hear the Word, but then worry, deceit and greed for the things of the world choke out the seed and prevent it from growing. They have too many other consuming demands in their life that don't leave room for the Word to grow.

Finally, the good soil provides the fertile environment where the Word can take root in the lives of those who hear it. Their seed grows and produces an abundant crop. While it may vary in quantity, their soil has produced healthy, plentiful fruit. This soil illustrates what happens when we cultivate and nurture the Word—we produce fruits of the Spirit.

So, how do we cultivate good soil in our lives so that we grow in the Spirit and produce good fruit? By infusing our dirt with the divine! Just as Jesus spit to make mud for the blind man's miracle, we must live in the fullness of the Holy Spirit and pour His power into the ground of our lives. When we allow the Word to take root in our lives, we experience His presence. As we get to know Him and grow in our relationship with Him, we discover He has the power to make miracles in the mess of the mundane. But we must give God access to our dirt before He grants us access to our destiny!

SCRIPTURE

"Blessed is the one . . . whose delight is in the law of the LORD, and who meditates on his law day and night. That person is like a tree planted by streams of water, which yields its fruit in season and whose leaf does not wither— whatever they do prospers" (Psalm 1:1–3).

Prayer

Heavenly Father, You have planted the seed of Your Word into the soil of my heart. May it continue to take root and be nourished by the example of Jesus and the power of the Holy Spirit. Please use the dirt in my life to produce Your fruit! Amen.

God's power fertilizes the soil of your mistakes, your flaws and your weaknesses to produce what you cannot grow on your own—the fruits of His Spirit!

When you surrender your soil to God's Spirit, God transforms you into the likeness of His perfect, holy Son. Right now, no matter what you may be facing, God is going to the beginning. God is returning to the original architectural design of humanity in order to align the original with the NOW. Where you are in your life and in your faith is where God meets you—*right now, right here!* Because Jesus came to save you, deliver you, heal you and reactivate His original plan for you.

Yes, God has a plan for you.

God has a plan for your children.

God has a plan for your children's children.

God has a plan for your now and for your next.

In God's original plan, you are not blind.

In God's original plan, you are not an addict.

In God's original plan, you are not an alcoholic.

In God's original plan, you are not broken.

In God's original plan, you are not full of anxiety.

In God's original plan, you are not the tail.

In God's original plan, you are not cursed.

In God's original plan, you are blessed!

You are not where you were.

You are not how you were.

You are not what others did to you.

You are not what you did to yourself.

You are who God says you are.

You are what God says you are.

You are an overcomer!

Christ followers have no other choice but to overcome. When the Holy Spirit is allowed to grow in all areas of your life, you flourish; you thrive like never before. You overcome all that has held you back. To overcome is to defeat, to conquer, to triumph over, to win!

There is nothing you cannot overcome, regardless of the muddy mess you're in now. Through the power of God's Spirit, you can overcome everything holding you back. What other people did to you. What other people have said about you. What you have falsely believed about yourself. What the world says about you. What the world does to you. Jesus said, "These things I have spoken to you, so that in Me you may have peace. In the world you have tribulation, but take courage; I have overcome the world" (John 16:33 NASB1995). Through the power of Christ in you, you cannot help but overcome anything that prevents you from being all God made you to be.

You are more than a conqueror—you are an *overcomer*!

SCRIPTURE

"But he said to me, 'My grace is sufficient for you, for my power is made perfect in weakness.' Therefore I will boast all the more gladly about my weaknesses, so that Christ's power may rest on me" (2 Corinthians 12:9).

Prayer

Dear God, through Your power, I am no longer stuck in the muddy messes of life! I give You glory, praise and honor for all the miraculous ways You are transforming my life. Keep my eyes open and focused on You. Amen.

Through the power of God's Spirit in you, there is nothing you cannot overcome!

God's power has always enabled His people to overcome. Throughout the Bible, we see it over and over again. This book is not the book of perfect people. This sacred text is not a historical categorization of pristine, unblemished, stainless saints. Without a doubt, from Genesis to Revelation, this is a book of overcomers!

Abraham overcame the lies—including his own.

Joseph overcame the pit and the betrayal of his own brothers.

Moses overcame his past, his temper and Pharaoh.

Joshua overcame the disobedience of his troops and his fear of being alone when his mentor died.

Gideon overcame the threshing floor.

Samson overcame his pride, his lack of respect for the anointing and Delilah's deception.

David overcame Saul's spear, a bear, a lion, a giant and his own moral turpitude.

Esther overcame the haters.

Daniel overcame the lions.

The Hebrew boys overcame the furnace.

Job overcame the loss of everything!

Peter overcame the cursing of his blessing.

Paul overcame the shipwreck and the snake.

And Jesus, the Son of God, incarnate here on earth to do for us what we could not do for ourselves—Jesus overcame darkness, death and defeat.

Jesus overcame everything!

So, now it's time to add your name to this list. Think for a moment about what you believe is holding you back in your faith—your past mistakes, your weaknesses, your wounds from others, everything and anything that you believe impedes your spiritual growth and the work of God's Spirit in your life. No matter what you might believe holds you back, this is the undeniable truth: *You are, in Christ, by Christ, for Christ, an overcomer!*

You have already overcome so much. You wouldn't be reading this right now if you hadn't overcome pain, sorrow, anger, fear, depression, anxiety and doubt. They may still creep in from time to time, like weeds trying to displace the blossom of faith in your life. But overcomers know how to get rid of weeds!

Just consider for a moment all the things in your life that you've overcome—especially those things that felt unbearable, unimaginable, intolerable at the time. Abuse, grief, trauma, poverty, bankruptcy, divorce, shame—they felt like they would destroy you. But they did not—you persevered, you trusted and you overcame!

Whether you overcame thirty years ago or thirty days ago or thirty minutes ago, you called on the name of the Lord and experienced the power of His Spirit in you. Do not let anything choke your growth as you mature in your faith. God has breathed new life into you through the Spirit. Jesus has entered into the muddy mess of your mistakes and missteps and washed you clean in His blood.

Open your eyes and see the new life inside you!

SCRIPTURE

"Therefore, since we are surrounded by such a great cloud of witnesses, let us throw off everything that hinders and the sin that so easily entangles. And let us run with perseverance the race marked out for us, fixing our eyes on Jesus, the pioneer and perfecter of faith" (Hebrews 12:1–2).

Prayer

Heavenly Father, You have graciously given me the gift of salvation through Your Son, Jesus, and the presence of Your Holy Spirit within me. Thank You for meeting me in the messiness and producing Your miraculous masterpiece in my life. Amen.

You may not realize how your biases create filters that distort your vision. If you want to see clearly, then it's time to consider the lenses coloring your view.

The way you interpret your life's events may be blinding you. The filter you create from your experiences, impressions, memories and perceptions color the way you view your identity, your purpose and your relationships—including how you view God. Simply put, you may have unknowingly and unintentionally developed false beliefs based on inaccurate assumptions, others' opinions, traumatic experiences and subjective bias that distort the truth of who God says you are, how He wants you to live and the purpose He created you to fulfill.

How did this filter begin to blind you? In psychology, *subjective bias* is the term used to describe the way participants in a study or experiment behave in ways to meet the expectations of those conducting the research. Essentially, it's a way of conforming and trying to perform well and get validation by giving those in charge what you think they want.

This same tendency operates on some level when you filter your way of seeing with those past messages you've internalized into beliefs. Think of it as a kind of self-fulfilling prophecy, a limited perspective that prevents you from seeing clearly and accurately. Instead of getting validation from researchers, though, you validate the false beliefs holding you prisoner, no matter how critical, inaccurate and unhealthy they may be. Simply put, your subjective bias prevents you from seeing the truth of God's perspective.

How have you experienced this kind of self-critical bias? What false beliefs do you struggle to shake? What negative assumptions and past experiences tend to blindside you when your circumstances don't turn out as expected?

Perhaps you didn't get the promotion you wanted, so you tell yourself that you're not surprised because you know you're not talented enough (or smart enough or whatever enough). You reinforce this false belief and likely make it more challenging for you to risk applying for a promotion in the future.

This kind of self-sabotaging trap might emerge in your relationships. You find yourself drawn to the same kind of person, who inevitably deceives and hurts you. Instead of realizing the cycle, however, you tell yourself that you must not deserve a healthy relationship. It might be your finances and how you handle debt. You falsely believe you're never going to have enough money, that you're always going to be in debt, so you don't follow a budget or monitor your spending habits. Basically, you only see what you want to see because the blinders of your past experiences shape your present expectations.

Until you face the truth about your false beliefs, though, you're blinding yourself to what God wants to do in you and through you.

SCRIPTURE

"For now we see only a reflection as in a mirror; then we shall see face to face. Now I know in part; then I shall know fully, even as I am fully known" (1 Corinthians 13:12).

—————————— *Prayer* ——————————

Dear Lord, I need You to show me the inaccurate filters and distorted lenses that have been obscuring my spiritual vision. Open my eyes to see You, God, so that I may know the truth of Your Word and the power of Your Spirit. Amen.

day

27

Do not allow your skeptics and critics to impede your ability to see what God is doing in you and in your life. Focus on what God is revealing before your very eyes!

The blind man Jesus healed likely harbored some false beliefs about himself. Because the Braille language had not yet been invented, this man, blind since birth, couldn't read and remained uneducated. His inability to read and lack of education might have led the people around him to assume he was not intelligent.

Based on how he responded after Jesus gave him the gift of sight, though, he was likely quite intelligent and a quick learner. In fact, he probably would have made an excellent attorney based on how he handled being interrogated by the Jewish religious leaders! Because he ended up sparring verbally with them not once, but *twice*.

The people who knew him as the blind beggar at first doubted it was the same man when they saw him newly sighted (John 9:9). When the man assured them he was, indeed, the person who had been blind since birth, they remained inquisitive, and some were likely skeptical. They wanted to know how the man regained his sight, and then when he told them, they wanted to know where Jesus was.

Since the man didn't know, this group of inquisitors took him before the Pharisees (John 9:13–17). Not surprisingly, they did not focus on the incredible miracle of the blind man receiving sight but on the fact that Jesus had healed him on the Sabbath, a religious day of rest with very strict rules of what one could and couldn't do under the Law of Moses.

Because the Pharisees remained uncertain about what to do with Jesus healing the blind man on a Sabbath, they doubted the miracle entirely and called for the man's parents so they could interrogate them as well (John 9:18–19). Talk about subjective bias and circular reasoning! The Pharisees were so intent on denying that Jesus was the Messiah that they looked for other ways to discredit the muddy miracle rather than even entertain the evidence before them. They refused to see the sighted man right in front of them!

You may experience the same with certain people in your life. As the Lord produces a miracle from your mess, these individuals will look for explanations, excuses and indictments but refuse to acknowledge the unlimited power of God's Spirit unleashed in your life. They work hard to remain skeptical, uncertain and disbelieving despite your testimony, in word and in deed, to the miraculous power of Jesus in your blind spots.

Do not be discouraged, distracted or derailed by such individuals. They cannot see what you can see now that your spiritual sight has been restored. Trust God to use you to display His power and glory as your miracle unfolds from your mess!

SCRIPTURE

"You are the light of the world. . . . Let your light shine before others, that they may see your good deeds and glorify your Father in heaven" (Matthew 5:14–16).

Prayer

Jesus, You are the Light of the world! I want to shine with the light of Your love so that others will know You and You alone are responsible for the miracle emerging from my mess. All glory and honor is Yours, Lord! Amen.

When others witness the miraculous impact of God's Spirit at work in your mess, they can choose to see the Source of your healing—or they can choose spiritual blindness.

The Pharisees didn't want to face the glory of God right in front of them. They wanted to hear this man parrot the falsehood they believed about the Healer—that Jesus was a sinner violating the religious law. But the clear-eyed man looking at them refused to be manipulated. The recipient of new sight not only refused—he stood up to these religious elitists and turned their own logic back on them:

> The man answered, "Now that is remarkable! You don't know where he comes from, yet he opened my

eyes. We know that God does not listen to sinners. He listens to the godly person who does his will. Nobody has ever heard of opening the eyes of a man born blind. If this man were not from God, he could do nothing."

To this they replied, "You were steeped in sin at birth; how dare you lecture us!" And they threw him out.

John 9:30–34

Notice the progressive sequence here. First, the man points out the hole in their attack—because it's basically irrelevant where the Healer came from. Knowing where Jesus was from—Nazareth, of course—still wouldn't explain why or how He was able to heal this man who had been blind since birth.

Then the man explained another line of reasoning. "Okay, we know God doesn't listen to sinners," he said, finding common ground with the Pharisees. "He listens to the godly person who does His will." In other words, if Jesus were a sinner—presumably of violating Sabbath law, as they claimed—then why would God work through Him?

The man then delivered the perfect closer: "Who's ever heard of anyone giving sight to a man born blind?

Only someone from God could do it! Otherwise, it wouldn't have worked." Without a rational rebuttal, the Pharisees resorted once again to attempting to discredit the man before them: "How dare you! You were conceived in sin—you have no authority to lecture us no matter how clearly right you may be."

Despite the fact that this man had testified to the miracle he himself experienced, despite the testimony of this man's parents, despite the second interrogation and this man's brilliant defense, the religious leaders closed their eyes even tighter. Rather than celebrate the miracle before them, rather than praise and worship God, rather than attempt to open their minds and hearts to the possibility that Jesus was the long-promised Messiah, the Pharisees chose blindness.

You, however, have chosen to receive the healing gift of spiritual sight.

You know the power of Jesus' healing touch in your life.

You are experiencing the power of His Spirit at work in your mess!

SCRIPTURE

"Jesus looked at them and said, 'With man this is impossible, but not with God; all things are possible with God" (Mark 10:27).

—————————— *Prayer* ——————————

Lord, thank You for using the messiness of my life to create a miracle that others cannot deny. What is impossible by human means is always possible for You. You are transforming my mistakes into Your masterpiece. Amen.

Circumstances may blindside you, but you don't have to remain in the dark. If you want to see clearly, you must be willing to worship while wounded!

If the healed man's story as told to us had ended when he went to the Pool of Siloam and came home seeing (John 9:7), or even after his neighbors and witnesses questioned him (John 9:8–12), then we might assume he more or less lived happily ever after. But clearly that's not what happened. Suddenly, this man's messy miracle became even messier as he realized he was in the crosshairs of his Healer's enemies.

Sometimes, even when you get your miracle, what follows radically departs from your expectations. You assume that once you can see clearly, everything

Walk Out of Your Mess

should be beautifully vivid and colorful, but then you open your eyes to a world of shade and shadows. You see not only what is beautiful and true, but also the harsh realities of sin and the lies of the enemy.

Perhaps you thought that after your miraculous recovery from cancer, you would do nothing but rejoice—and then the medical bills come in and the debt collectors start calling. You expected that once your marriage had been healed by the power of God's Spirit, your spouse would love you exactly like you want to be loved—only to discover old habits still linger. It might be that you finally got out of debt through an unexpected windfall from heaven—only to be grounded by the expense of replacing the roof on your house.

Just as the Pharisees couldn't stand to give Jesus credit for the blind man's miracle of sight, the enemy will look for opportunities to drag your miracle back into the mud. The devil will try to trigger old scripts and old responses, making you doubt your miracle and question the extent of God's power. The painful labels and stinging criticism of past haters will resurface as the enemy employs every method at his disposal to cloud your spiritual vision.

When this happens, you must keep your eyes open to the holy mess before you.

Even if it's not what you expected—*especially* when it's not what you expected—you must trust God to meet you when you're still hurting after the miracle.

That's when you embrace the tension of worshiping while wounded.

Opening your eyes to a holy mess requires you to worship the holy while grieving the mess. That's basically the essence of faith in action! The people who will change the world are born-again believers following Jesus Christ. They are disciples of the risen Christ who know who He is even in the midst of their pain. Those who are certain of His identity even in the midst of their suffering.

Choose to worship Jesus even in the midst of your mess, while waiting on your miracle, and then after your miracle happens!

SCRIPTURE

"Praise the LORD, my soul; all my inmost being, praise his holy name. Praise the LORD, my soul, and forget not all his benefits—who forgives all your sins and heals all your diseases" (Psalm 103:1–3).

———————— *Prayer* ————————

Dear God, give me strength and patience when I'm weary and wounded. My desire is to praise Your holy name no matter what my circumstances may be! Today, I choose to worship in my woundedness and trust You to meet me right where I am. Amen.

When the circumstances of life leave you broken and battered, don't lose sight of the hope you have in Jesus. Stop looking at today's problems and start focusing on future promises!

Sometimes God covers our eyes now in order for us to open them later for what's next. When Jesus healed the man blind from birth, He spit on the ground and made mud, which He then spread over the blind man's eyes (John 9:6). In essence, Jesus blinded him to his own blindness. He placed the messy mask of the miraculous over this man's eyes in order to help him see the glory of God waiting for him ahead.

In order to experience the tension of your holy mess, you must adjust your vision.

Simply put, take your eyes off today's problems and open your eyes to tomorrow's promises.

When you're struggling, your pain can often blind you to the truth of God's promises. Because of what you can't see now, you struggle to glimpse the miracle that lies ahead. It's similar to a scientific double-blind study, in which neither participants nor researchers know which subjects are in the test groups and which are in the control groups. These studies are set up this way usually to prevent bias and expectations from affecting results. When it comes to matters of faith, though, holding on to hope in the harshness of life is essential.

When you suffer loss, injury, betrayal or disease, you may feel powerless and uncertain of how to go forward. You may wonder if God knows what He's doing. If He understands the depths of your pain. And if so, then why has He permitted this to happen? You feel like you're caught in a double blind, unable to see your present and unable to see your future.

But sometimes you have to go *through* to get *to*.

Sometimes you have to walk with your mess to get to your miracle.

Sometimes you have to experience what feels like death before you rise again.

Just like Lazarus, you will come out of your tomb and throw off your grave clothes! It feels messy and awkward and uncomfortable when you're coming back to life, walking in the mess to get to your miracle. But there's an expiration date on what you're going through. What you see now is not what you will see ahead. Remember that where you are is not where you are going!

When your praise speaks louder than your pain, nothing can stop you.

When your integrity is more important than your influence, nothing can stop you.

When you are driven by anointing rather than ambition, nothing can stop you!

When your hunger for righteousness is greater than your fear of criticism, nothing can stop you.

Wash away the mud from your eyes and step into the glorious future God has for you!

SCRIPTURE

"For our present troubles are small and won't last very long. Yet they produce for us a glory that vastly outweighs them and will last forever!" (2 Corinthians 4:17 NLT).

————————— *Prayer* —————————

Lord, help me not to lose sight of Your promises when the mud of life's messes obscures my ability to see Your miracle. Give me strength to persevere and faith to trust You. Amen.

Cleaning your heart and clearing your vision requires obedience, choosing to follow God's instructions to access His promises. Obedience requires being attuned to the Holy Spirit!

Water provides us with a multitude of benefits.

Physically, water helps us wash our bodies by eliminating dirt, grime, germs and bacteria from our skin, hair and nails. Many people appreciate the effects that water, whether hot or cold, has on their circulation and overall health. Others like the way water can stimulate and awaken their senses, while likely just as many enjoy the way water can relax them. Smelling clean and pleasant also facilitates social interactions and close relationships.

The psychological benefits of bathing are likely related to an awareness of both the health and social advantages. In certain areas of the world, bathing and showering, let alone having hot water to do so, are often a luxury. After camping, hiking, working out or doing physical labor, most people enjoy the relaxing, invigorating sensation of water cascading over their bodies. Being clean can have emotional benefits, too, leaving bathers feeling refreshed, renewed and restored.

The benefits of water are not limited to cleaning our bodies. Throughout the pages of Scripture, we find the cleansing power of water is spiritual as well. Water, like fire, can be either destructive and overwhelming or a life-giving, precious commodity. In the Old Testament, we see Noah obey God and survive the Flood, while Elijah endures a drought through God's provision before divine rains restore the land. In the New Testament, we find Jesus, and Peter briefly, walking on water, as well as Paul shipwrecked by a storm.

We also find water used to wash away the miraculous mud from the eyes of the man blind since birth. After spitting on the ground, making mud and applying a mask of it over the man's eyes, Jesus said, "Go, wash in the Pool of Siloam" (John 9:7). John's account of this messy miracle also informs us that Siloam means "Sent," as in the water sent forth into this pool. But the pool's name is no coincidence because Jesus sent this man out to complete his miracle, and the man obeyed—and came home seeing! Instead of existing as if his life were washed up, this man washed up and saw the new life before him.

The blind man had no logical reason to obey this stranger's instruction, especially considering how strange it must have been as Jesus made mud from dirt and spit and placed it over the man's sightless eyes. Yet a spark of hope might have been lit as well—why else would the blind man be told to go and wash unless something was about to happen? Washing his eyes with water completed the messy miracle in his midst.

What's the difference between being washed up and washing up? *Obedience!*

If you want to experience God's miracle in your mess, obey the voice of His Spirit.

SCRIPTURE

"If you love me, keep my commands. And I will ask the Father, and he will give you another advocate to help you and be with you forever—the Spirit of truth" (John 14:15–17).

— *Prayer* —

Dear God, thank You for the gift of Your Living Water that quenches the spiritual thirst within my soul. Empower me to remain obedient to Your instructions and to trust You, even when I cannot discern the miracle You are making from my mess. Amen.

day
32

> God is looking for people who trust Him more than those who understand Him. Faith is trusting God enough to obey Him now and prepare for your next!

If Jesus' command to go and wash in the Pool of Siloam surprised or confused the blind man, he didn't question it or demand an explanation. No, he simply obeyed and was healed! Perhaps he recognized the kindness, compassion and spiritual authority in the One speaking to him. Without even thinking about it, the blind man may have realized Who was standing before him because his soul recognized God's voice.

Knowing the sound of our Shepherd's voice is vitally important if we want to experience the fulfillment of our messy miracles in life. Jesus said, "My sheep listen to my voice; I know them, and they follow me" (John 10:27). Christ reminds us here that whoever has your ear will inevitably have your heart. When we're young and immature, we usually worry about who's talking about us, what they think, what they posted on social media, how they're influencing others.

As we mature and grow wiser, however, we learn to no longer care what others may say about us. We learn to care about whom we allow to speak into our lives. We learn to guard our hearts and minds in order to take our thoughts captive to Christ so that we may focus on matters of the Spirit. We realize we cannot grant heart access to just anyone. We learn to discern! Access should be limited to people of integrity who can handle both the blessed and the broken you.

You don't need someone else's permission to accept God's promises!

You don't need to understand God, and you don't need to make sense of God.

You need to *trust* God.

You need to *obey* God.

God is looking for people who trust Him more than those who understand Him.

Faith is trusting God when life makes no sense!

What you hear in the Spirit is more important than what you see in the flesh.

Jesus told the blind man, "Go wash yourself!" Again, we know Christ could instantly have healed this man, so why spit, make mud, cover his eyes and then tell him to go wash himself in the Pool of Sent? Because there are things you have to do by yourself, for yourself. Yes, it's good if someone can help, but sometimes in life you have to learn to pray, praise and prophesy for yourself.

You cannot ride others' coattails to praise the One healing you!

You cannot jump on the bandwagon of someone else's breakthrough!

There are decisions you cannot delegate.

There are actions you cannot appropriate.

Go wash yourself!

Do your part to complete the miracle God is working in your life.

SCRIPTURE

"We demolish arguments and every pretension that sets itself up against the knowledge of God, and we take captive every thought to make it obedient to Christ" (2 Corinthians 10:5).

Prayer

Good Shepherd, I recognize Your voice, and I obey Your instruction. Thank You for giving me ears to hear and eyes to see beyond my human capabilities. Help me to take all my thoughts captive to You so that I may be more like Jesus. Amen.

Experiencing God's miracle in your mess means walking by faith and not by sight. When life's storms swirl around you, keep your eyes fixed on Jesus—not your own abilities.

Of all the disciples mentioned in the New Testament, perhaps none better reflects both the conflicting emotions and passionate faith that we all experience at various times than Simon Peter. Drawing a blade to defend Jesus when the Roman soldiers came to arrest Him in the Garden of Gethsemane (John 18:10–11), Peter proceeded to deny even knowing Christ—not once, but three times—only hours later (Luke 22:54–62). Peter, like everyone at one time or another, suffered from impaired vision.

After teaching and feeding the five-thousand-plus in attendance, Jesus had sent His disciples ahead to the other side of the Sea of Galilee because He needed to spend some time in prayer alone (Matthew 14:22–24). They obeyed their Master when a storm came up and literally rocked their boat. When Jesus then tried to join them, Peter struggled with what he saw—was that a ghost on the water?

Jesus then told them not to be afraid because "it is I" (Matthew 14:27). He understandably assumed they would recognize His voice even if they couldn't see Him clearly because of the darkness. Apparently, though, Peter still wasn't entirely convinced, so he came up with an impromptu test that only Jesus could fulfill: "Lord, if it's you, tell me to come to you on the water" (v. 28). Notice that Peter didn't ask for Jesus to prove Himself by illuminating His face, stopping the wind or hopping in their boat with them. Instead, Peter wanted Jesus to empower him to do what the Lord Himself was doing—walking on water!

Jesus commanded Peter to come out of the boat toward Him, and so Peter did just that. But it didn't take long for Peter to lose sight of his Master and to lose the supernatural power sustaining his footsteps on the waves: "when he saw the wind, he was afraid and, beginning to sink" (Matthew 14:30).

Peter's experience likely reflects your own. When you're feeling uncertain, anxious and afraid, perhaps you ask God to give you a sign and pray that He will empower you to do something impossible. Then when the Lord gives you His power, you step out of your boat and begin walking on water. Before long, though, just like Peter, you see the wind.

When we choose to be a wind watcher, we allow ourselves to be overwhelmed by what our senses tell us. This is a natural human reaction to most adverse circumstances—but we still have a choice, just like Peter. We can give in and live according to what our senses tell us, or we can continue walking by faith even when life gets harder.

SCRIPTURE

"When hard pressed, I cried to the LORD; he brought me into a spacious place. The LORD is with me; I will not be afraid" (Psalm 118:5–6).

Prayer

Father God, when my mess gets muddier and the storms of life frighten me, let me listen for Your voice and trust You more than I trust my human senses, intellect or emotions. Bolster my courage that I may get out of my boat and walk by faith toward You. Amen.

day
34

When your spiritual vision has been restored, you can't take your eyes off Jesus! Worship is the only response worthy of the One who loves you and died for you.

The blind man whom Jesus healed not only received sight for his eyes—he developed spiritual vision as well. Because once Jesus revealed Himself as the Son of Man, how did the man respond? "'Master, I believe,' the man said, and worshiped him" (John 9:38 MSG). Instead of worshiping Christ, however, the Pharisees heard the exchange between Jesus and the miracle man and asked, "Does that mean you're calling us blind?" (John 9:40 MSG).

Instead of seeing Jesus for who He is, the Son of God, these unrepentant religious leaders saw only what they wanted to see—a threat to their power, whom they feared and hated. They refused to look again and open their eyes. They remained blind while the man who had been born blind was granted double vision! He received the gift of healthy eyes and the gift of faith in the Giver of that gift. This man knew when to stand up—before the Pharisees—and when to bow down—before Christ the Lord. This man learned to open his eyes and see, and who he saw resulted in worship. He didn't care what the Pharisees thought of him or what they might do to him. All he cared about was worshiping Jesus!

When you experience the power, peace and joy in your messy miracle, you open your eyes and worship. You worship in the midst of your wounds, you rejoice in the midst of your ruckus, and you praise through your problems. You sing in the desert because you know you will dance in the Promised Land. With the psalmist you proclaim, "Oh come, let us worship and bow down; let us kneel before the LORD, our Maker" (Psalm 95:6 ESV).

When you bow before God, you can stand before man.

When you kneel with conviction, you can stand up to conquer.

When you begin the day on your knees, you will finish the day on your feet.

When you open your eyes to worship, God will reveal His presence anew.

The Bible assures us that "faith comes by hearing, and hearing by the word of God" (Romans 10:17 NKJV). Now is not the time to listen to the Pharisees doubting the power of Jesus even when confronted with the walking miracle you demonstrate in their midst. Now is not the time to listen to gossips and gabbers who speculate about who Jesus is when you already know He is the Son of God, the Prince of Peace, Emmanuel, the Messiah, your Lord and Savior. Now is not the time to look at the wind or listen to the voice of fear in your mind. Now is the time to fall on your knees before the King of kings!

Unconditional worship is the only appropriate response when you see Jesus!

SCRIPTURE

"Give praise to the LORD, proclaim his name; make known among the nations what he has done. Sing to him, sing praise to him; tell of all his wonderful acts" (Psalm 105:1–2).

Prayer

Dear God, my soul sings out to You with thanks and praise! Like the blind man whom Jesus healed, allow me to see the truth of who You really are. Let my life be a triumphant testimony to Your miraculous power in the midst of my mess. Amen.

> You are no longer who you once were. In Jesus,
> through Jesus, with Jesus, because of Jesus, the new
> you is alive and well!

Once you experience God's presence in your life, your
eyes are opened to the fact that you are no longer
who you once were. You are a new creature in Christ!
You are no longer a mess-maker, mud-tracker or dirt-
wallower—you are washed clean as snow. You can see
what you once could not see, including your new identity as a child of God.

You recall that when Jesus and His disciples first
noticed the man blind since birth, the disciples asked
the cause of his blindness—was it the man's sin or the
sin of his parents? But Jesus immediately clarified that

neither was at fault (John 9:3–5). Instead, the man's blindness was an opportunity for the power of God to be showcased so that His glory might be revealed. Then Christ seized this perfectly timed moment to provide the ultimate visual aid to illustrate what He had just told His followers. Rather than being caused by anyone's sin, Jesus indicated the man's blindness served as a revelatory reality to spotlight God's power in action.

It's noteworthy as well that Jesus said nothing directly to the blind man—not until after He caked miraculous mud over his eyes and told him to go wash in the Pool of Siloam (John 9:7). Curiously enough, the blind man did not object, did not question why this stranger was placing mud over his sightless eyes, did not ask the stranger's identity, did not try to stop the very personal action being perpetrated on him. The blind man's silent response in itself demonstrated faith in God, particularly since we can assume he had just heard what Jesus told His disciples.

There are times when we miss out on the messy miracle being performed in our midst because it doesn't arrive in the manner we expect. Rather than silently receiving the mud we must endure before we wash our eyes and see anew, we resist the mud altogether. Or we don't understand why and how God is doing what He's doing so we step back when the Spirit tries to touch us with holy power. We fail to recognize that having faith in God means surrendering the limitations of our human perspective and trusting His omnipotent, omniscient vantage.

Once we surrender our tendency to rely on our human senses and faculties, however, we begin to see with the eyes of our heart. We recognize Jesus' presence in our lives through the power of the Holy Spirit. We discover that we are not who we once thought we were. We have been forgiven, healed and unleashed to be the person God created us to be!

SCRIPTURE

"For you are a people holy to the LORD your God. The LORD your God has chosen you out of all the peoples on the face of the earth to be his people, his treasured possession" (Deuteronomy 7:6).

Prayer

Dear Lord, You have removed the layers of dirt and grime from my heart and washed me clean through the blood of Jesus. Remind me that I am no longer who I once was—let me experience the fullness of who I am in Christ! Amen.

Receiving God's miracle in your mess requires a willing-ness to rise above old ways and embrace who you are in Christ. You must leave the familiarity of mud if you want to walk on water!

You must realize that wanting to experience God's mir-acle in your mess requires stepping out in faith—and embracing the consequences. Once your sight has been restored and the mud washed away, you will never see yourself, other people or God the same way you once saw them. You will experience the peace, purpose and passion that comes from having the Holy Spirit living within you!

The man who had been blind experienced this radi-cal change, but there was another man with a physical disability who encountered Jesus' healing presence with life-changing results. This man had a physical limitation as well—instead of his sight, however, he had lost the full use of his legs for 38 years. Jesus, on His way to Jerusalem for one of the Jewish festivals, saw this man lying near the Sheep Gate of the Temple close to the pool known as Bethesda and learned of his condition. Rather than introduce Himself or make mud pies, Christ simply asked the man, "Do you want to get well?" (John 5:1–6).

Now, such an obvious question may seem unnecessary or even a cruel taunt if it had been asked by anyone other than Jesus. The man's reason for being there would have been obvious to those all around him. This particular pool was well known for its miraculous healing power after the water would bubble up, presumably when stirred supernaturally by an angel. Crowds of people wanting to be healed—including the blind, the lame, the paralyzed—gathered and waited on the colonnade porches to be the first in the water and experience healing (John 5:4). Clearly, if this man was lying there along with so many others in need, he wanted to be well. Otherwise, why bother to be there, right?

Which brings us back to Jesus' question—why ask something so seemingly obvious? Aside from what He observed with His eyes in the situation, the Son of God knew the desires of this man's heart. And yet Christ still chose to ask the man deliberately, *"Do you want to get well?"*

We can safely assume Jesus wasn't being unkind to this man. We can also recognize that our Lord was not merely making conversation or chatting to be polite. Jesus intentionally asked this question because its relevance remains timeless. This apparently obvious question is one we must answer for ourselves when we, too, encounter His miraculous power in the midst of our mess. The answer may seem clear, but when we receive our messy miracle, our lives will never be the same.

Will you relinquish the familiarity of your mess in order to experience the fullness of God's miracle in your life?

SCRIPTURE

"You were taught, with regard to your former way of life, to put off your old self, which is being corrupted by its deceitful desires; to be made new in the attitude of your minds; and to put on the new self, created to be like God in true righteousness and holiness" (Ephesians 4:22–24).

─────────────── *Prayer* ───────────────

Heavenly Father, thank You for creating me in Your image and conforming me to the likeness of Your Son, Jesus. I surrender my old self and leave it behind in the muddy mess of the past and embrace the new life You have given me in Christ. Amen.

day

37

If you want to experience God's miracle out of your mess, then you must risk venturing beyond your comfort zone. As you trust God with all areas of your life, you discover what a difference His presence makes.

Miracles in our messes require our participation. We're often passively waiting on God and blaming our suffering on what we lack, on other people, on bad timing. But what if God is waiting on us to stand up, pick up our mat, and walk?

The lame man had been waiting and waiting and waiting—for 38 years—and no one had come through for him (John 5:1–6). He presumably still harbored hope because, after all, he kept coming to the pool there, and it seems logical that he blamed his ongoing suffering on his inability. He viewed his healing as

157

conditional on variables beyond his control. Getting there with his mat and waiting for the waters to bubble was the best he thought he could do.

But then Jesus intervened.

Asking if the man wanted to be well.

Christ is asking you the same question, "Do you want to be well?"

Do you want My miracle in the midst of your mess?

Do you want My Spirit unleashed in your life?

Do you want to open your eyes to the new you?

No matter what your circumstances may be right now, you have choices.

You can remain in a victim mindset, or you can embrace the healing power of the Holy Spirit in your life. There's also the option to believe you can control your circumstances by your own power, trying harder and doing more, exhausting yourself as you eventually face your own limitations.

You have to be willing to leave the old you behind.

This departure sounds easier to do than it is to complete. Most of us gravitate toward that which is familiar and comfortable. As long as God allows us to stay within our comfort zone, we have no problem remaining faithful and obedient. When the Lord calls us into new territory, though, our trepidation often leads to hesitation. We fear the unknown because our imagination begins working overtime to come up with worst-case scenarios. Rather than trust God and step forward, we often get stuck in place. We know we can't go back, and yet our fears prevent us from going forward.

But God loves you too much to allow you to remain in the mud.

He loves you too much to allow you to get stuck in past mistakes.

Your Creator wants you to thrive and flourish, to grow and blossom in order to bring to life all that He has placed within you. But you must do your part. In order for God to complete His miracle in your mess, you have to invite Him into every area of your life.

SCRIPTURE

"For we know that our old self was crucified with him so that the body ruled by sin might be done away with, that we should no longer be slaves to sin—because anyone who has died has been set free from sin" (Romans 6:6–7).

Prayer

Dear God, search my heart as I surrender it to You so that Your Holy Spirit abides in all areas of my life. Remind me that I am no longer bound by sin but liberated by grace. Your mercy and lovingkindness have transformed my life! Amen.

day

38

When you slip in the muddy mess of the past, don't wallow in who you used to be. Stand in the fullness of your new identity in Christ and walk by faith!

As you experience God's miracle in your mess, you will likely encounter the tension of transition between the old you and the new you, the blind you and the healed you, who sees more clearly than ever. The old you, the messy you, remains mired in the past, trying to blind you to the truth, leaving you flailing as the broken you, the fallen you, the sinful you, the fleshly you, the depressed and anxious you, the cursed you, the empty you, the victim you, the dead you.

The new you, however, sees the truth and knows who you really are. The new you views your identity the way God sees you, as the forgiven you, the born-again you, the saved you, the delivered you, the baptized you, the healed you, the bought and redeemed you, the blessed, favored, and anointed you. With open eyes and an open heart, this you knows who you are in Christ, the blood-washed, Jesus-following, Bible-based, Spirit-filled, Father-loved, devil-rebuking, temptation-resisting, righteousness-pursuing you. Through the power of Christ and your relationship with His Spirit, you are now the chosen you, the prophetic you, the conquering you, the ruling and reigning you, the sanctified you, the thriving and growing, glorious you.

As the reality of God's miracle in your mess unfolds in your life, you must remember what is true about you.

The old you is dead and buried.

The old you will never come back!

You are not who you used to be—no matter how you feel or what your circumstances may be. The old you died with Jesus and has now been reborn through the power of His resurrection. In Jesus, through Jesus, with Jesus, because of Jesus, *the new you is alive and well!*

Consider the contrast Paul made, "If the old way, which brings condemnation, was glorious, how much more glorious is the new way, which makes us right with God! In fact, that first glory was not glorious at all compared with the overwhelming glory of the new way" (2 Corinthians 3:9–10 NLT).

While the old you glimpsed the promise, the new you will possess it.

While the old you complained, the new you will conquer.

While the old you hoped for glory, the new you will see God's glory!

You are no longer the you mired in the mess, blind and unable to see who you are and where you're going. You are in a new day, a new season, with a new song.

Your new identity in Christ is no secret!

Open your eyes to the power of who God has made you to be!

SCRIPTURE

"Brothers and sisters, I do not consider myself yet to have taken hold of it. But one thing I do: Forgetting what is behind and straining toward what is ahead, I press on toward the goal to win the prize for which God has called me heavenward in Christ Jesus" (Philippians 3:13–14).

Prayer

Lord Jesus, as I experience the tension of transitioning into the fullness of my identity in You, remind me of what's ahead and not what's behind. Give me patience to wait on Your timing and to trust in Your plans for revealing Your miracle in my mess. Amen.

Walking by faith requires us to recognize our Savior's voice through the whisper of the Holy Spirit in us. Guided by His wisdom, we surrender our limitations and trust His direction.

When we follow our Good Shepherd, when we have the Holy Spirit living in us, we learn to recognize the sound of our Savior's voice just as well as the blind man whom Jesus healed heard it that day. As we see clearly and listen closely, we rely on the Spirit and experience Jesus' presence all around us—in the stunning beauty of creation, in the lives of other people and in the miracles in our midst.

When we follow our Master's voice, we may need to take a second look, or a third or a twenty-third for that matter, but we can't miss His presence right in front of us. As our spiritual eyes grow accustomed to looking through a divine lens and seeing God's eternal perspective, we realize there's so much more going on than meets our mortal eyes. We no longer get discouraged when we don't get what we expected.

We remember that God is always at work in our lives, whether we see it—or see it the way we expect to see it—or not. Paul expressed this desire for clear vision to early believers at Ephesus: "I pray that the eyes of your heart may be enlightened in order that you may know the hope to which he has called you, the riches of his glorious inheritance in his holy people, and his incomparably great power for us who believe" (Ephesians 1:18–19).

God's Word makes the contrast between what we see with our eyes and what we see with the eyes of our heart even sharper: "As we look not to the things that are seen but to the things that are unseen. For the things that are seen are transient, but the things that are unseen are eternal" (2 Corinthians 4:18 ESV). Learning to open our eyes and see beyond what our human eyes register occurs as we mature in our faith: "For we walk by faith, not by sight" (2 Corinthians 5:7 ESV).

Growing stronger in our trust in the Lord, we refuse to get stuck in the mud or lost in the messiness of life. We rely on the Holy Spirit, not merely our human senses, to guide us on the path of righteousness as we fulfill our divine purpose. As God transforms our mess into His miracle, we celebrate by giving Him thanks and praise for doing what cannot be done by human means.

And when Jesus asks us the same question that He asked this once-blind man, "I'm right in front of you! Don't you know My voice when you hear it?", we answer in similar fashion: *"You are my Lord and Master, and I trust You fully."*

SCRIPTURE

"My sheep listen to my voice; I know them, and they follow me. I give them eternal life, and they shall never perish; no one will snatch them out of my hand" (John 10:27–28).

Prayer

My beloved Savior, allow me to hear Your voice and glimpse Your presence amid the messiness, busyness and craziness of life. Allow me to draw closer to You as I trust You more fully and grow in my faith. Amen.

day
40

> You cannot embrace what God has for you until you
> first accept what God did for you. Once you see by
> the power of God's Spirit, your entire perspective
> changes!

How you see spiritually is a matter of perspective just
as much as the way you see physically relies on your
vantage point. Photographers and visual artists know
that perspective in their work depends in large part
on the position of their lenses and their expanse. Di-
mensionality depends on showing depth and texture,
with sharpness of clarity moving from the background
to the foreground.

Some images are designed to illustrate this dynamic,
subjective tension in how viewers see them. Optical
illusions and 3-D puzzles may seem to shift between

different images right before your eyes, one moment revealing a certain image until your vision adjusts and assimilates another. One moment, you see an ornate vase occupying the forefront of a picture; the next, your vision shifts and glimpses the profiles of two people staring at one another. The shift depends on how you interpret the negative space, the empty space around and between the subjects on which you choose to focus.

The way you live out your faith works much the same way.

You can experience your life based on the sensory data collected and collated by your human faculties—many people do. They rely on their intellect to process and proceed based on what they see, hear, smell, taste and touch. If they can't see it or hear it or sense it, then they falsely believe it doesn't exist. Living by this kind of vision largely remains stationary, one-dimensional and fixated on negative space. There's no miracle—just an ongoing mess!

Or you can shift your sight from negative space to positive faith and experience your life based on your relationship with the holy and almighty, living God through the gift of His Son, Jesus, and the power of His

Holy Spirit. You can live like the saints of Scripture, those pioneers of faith, both named and unnamed, who chose to trust God more than their human senses. Like the man born blind who felt the Son of God place mud on his face in order that he might receive the gift of sight, you can experience the unprecedented joy of a messy miracle.

If you're struggling to see clearly, then remember: Perception is not reality.

It may look like the enemy is winning.

It may feel like you're stuck in place.

But God's grace is all you need—His power works best in weakness.

When you are weak, then you are strong in the power of the Spirit.

By His grace, you are saved.

By His wounds, you are healed.

By His love, you are transformed.

Your messy miracle has already started!

So wash away the mud.

Open your eyes.

Shift your perspective to the eternal.

And watch what God will do!

SCRIPTURE

"Being confident of this, that he who began a good work in you will carry it on to completion until the day of Christ Jesus" (Philippians 1:6).

———— *Prayer* ————

Loving Father, I praise You for meeting me in the messiness of my life and producing Your miracle! Thank You for the gift of Your Spirit, who dwells in me and reminds me to look beyond what my eyes may see as I focus on Jesus. Amen.

Samuel Rodriguez is president of the National Hispanic Christian Leadership Conference (NHCLC), the world's largest Hispanic Christian organization, with more than 42,000 U.S. churches and many additional churches spread throughout the Spanish-speaking diaspora.

Rodriguez stands recognized by CNN, Fox News, Univision and Telemundo as America's most influential Latino/Hispanic faith leader. *Charisma* magazine named him one of the forty leaders who changed the world. The *Wall Street Journal* named him one of the top-twelve Latino leaders, and he was the only faith leader on that list. He has been named among the "Top 100 Christian Leaders in America" (*Newsmax* 2018) and nominated as one of the "100 Most Influential People in the World" (*Time* 2013). Rodriguez is regularly featured on CNN, Fox News, Univision, PBS, *Christianity Today*, the *New York Times*, the *Wall Street Journal* and many others.

Rodriguez was the first Latino to deliver the keynote address at the annual Martin Luther King Jr. Commemorative Service at Ebenezer Baptist Church, and he is a recipient of the Martin Luther King Jr. Leadership Award presented by the Congress of Racial Equality.

Rodriguez advised former American presidents Bush, Obama and Trump, and he frequently consults with Congress regarding advancing immigration and criminal justice reform as well as religious freedom and pro-life initiatives. By the grace of God, Reverend Samuel Rodriguez is one of the few individuals to have participated in the inauguration ceremonies of two different presidents representing both political parties.

In January 2009, Pastor Sam read from the gospel of Luke for Mr. Obama's inaugural morning service at Saint John's Episcopal Church. On January 20, 2017, at Mr. Trump's inauguration, with more than one billion people watching from around the world, Pastor Sam became the first Latino evangelical to participate in a U.S. presidential inaugural ceremony, reading from Matthew 5 and concluding with "in Jesus' name!" In April 2020, Reverend Rodriguez was appointed to the National Coronavirus Recovery Commission to offer specialized experience and expertise in crisis mitigation and recovery to help national, state and local leaders guide America through the COVID-19 pandemic.

Rodriguez is the executive producer of two films: *Breakthrough*, the GMA Dove Award winner for

Inspirational Film of the Year, with an Academy Award nomination for Best Original Song, and *Flamin' Hot*, in partnership with Franklin Entertainment and 20th Century Fox. He is also co-founder of TBN Salsa, an international Christian-based broadcast television network, and he is the author of *You Are Next, Shake Free, Be Light*—a number-one *L.A. Times* bestseller—and *From Survive to Thrive*, a number-one Amazon bestseller.

He earned his master's degree from Lehigh University and has received honorary doctorates from Northwest, William Jessup and Baptist University of the Americas.

Rodriguez serves as the senior pastor of New Season Church, one of America's fastest-growing megachurches and number thirteen on Newsmax's Top 50 megachurches in America, with campuses in Los Angeles and Sacramento, California, where he resides with his wife, Eva, and their three children.

For more information, please visit:

www.PastorSam.com

RevSamuelRodriguez

@pastorsamuelrodriguez

@nhclc